# ORGANIZATIONAL DOCUMENTS:
# A GUIDE FOR PARTNERSHIPS AND PROFESSIONAL CORPORATIONS

## By Mark F. Murray, J.D.

### Issued by the Management of an Accounting Practice Committee

**American Institute of Certified Public Accountants**

1 2 3 4 5 6 7 8 9 0    IPM    9 9 8 7 6 5 4 3 2 1 0

The sample incorporation sequence appearing on pages 64 through 66 was adapted with permission from *Professional Corporations Handbook*, published and copyrighted by Commerce Clearing House, Inc., 4025 W. Peterson Ave., Chicago, Illinois 60646.

**Library of Congress Cataloging-in-Publication Data**

Murray, Mark F.
    Organizational documents : a guide for partnerships and
    professional corporations /Mark F. Murray.
       p.  cm.
    Includes index.
    ISBN 0–87051–089–4
    1. Accounting firms—United States.  2. Partnership—United
    States—Forms.  3. Incorporation—United States—Forms.
I. American Institute of Certified Public Accountants.  II. Title.
HF5627.M87  1990                      90–1095
657'.068—dc20                         CIP

# Foreword

MAP publications are designed as educational and reference material for members of the AICPA and others interested in practice management. They are intended to provide practitioners with up-to-date guidance on aspects of firm management.

Well-drafted partnership agreements and incorporation documents are the basis for effective firm operations—the foundation of successful firms. With the necessary organizational documents in place, members of your firm know what is expected of them and what to expect from the firm.

Whether you practice as a partnership or professional corporation, your organizational documents should reflect your firm's management style and professional goals. This book will help you and your partners fully participate in the process of drafting your firm's partnership agreement or incorporation documents. You will be better able to work in concert with your attorney to draft documents that are suited to the special needs and goals of your firm.

In July 1990, the AICPA Board of Directors approved for submission to the AICPA Council a proposal to permit members of the AICPA to practice as limited liability corporations. The proposal will be discussed at the Fall 1990 Council meeting and, if approved, will be submitted to the full membership by mail ballot. The results of the ballot should be known by the spring of 1991. If the proposal is approved by the membership, members should know that most state statutes now permit CPA firms to practice only as partnerships or professional corporations which impose unlimited liability on those involved with the engagement. The AICPA will keep members informed of developments. The Management of an Accounting Practice Committee will communicate news on this issue in *The Practicing CPA*.

LOUIS J. BARBICH
*Chairman*
*Management of an Accounting*
*Practice Committee*

NANCY MYERS
*Director*
*Industry and Practice*
*Management Division*

# Preface

This book is intended to help you prepare partnership agreements and incorporation documents and to provide you with a summary of concepts that are involved in this process. IT IS NOT INTENDED TO PROVIDE LEGAL ADVICE OR TO SERVE AS A LEGAL FORM. Rather, it demonstrates that the active participation of legal counsel is essential. Since the planning and creation of an accounting practice and its organizational documents involve both detailed personal and technical issues, the combined involvement of you, your partners, and a competent attorney should improve your firm's prospects for success.

This book is divided into four sections:

- Section I discusses factors to consider when you decide which business entity is appropriate for your accounting practice. It includes a chart that identifies and compares the foremost business characteristics to consider when making this decision.

- Section II begins with an overview of partnership agreements, followed by a discussion of the reasons for partners' reluctance to prepare a partnership agreement as well as the objectives of a well-drafted agreement. This section concludes with a collection of sample provisions from which you can choose. The sample agreement not only assists in outlining a partnership agreement, but it also serves as a checklist to determine the effectiveness of an existing one. The agreement is suitable for firms of all sizes, although it may prove most valuable to small- and medium-size firms.

- Section III opens with a discussion of the documents involved in the incorporation of an accounting practice and identifies issues addressed by each agreement. The section continues with an examination of the roles and responsibilities of the members of a professional corporation and the mandatory procedures that help ensure your corporate status. The section concludes with a step-by-step approach to incorporating. (The appendixes contain sample documents).

- Section IV examines the integral role of both the accountant and the attorney in matters dealing with the organization of an accounting practice. Featured in this section are discussions of the Uniform Partnership Act (UPA), the Model Business Corporation Act (MBCA), controlling statutes and decisions, as well as the manner in which conflicts among these bodies can be prevented or resolved.

Once you have read this book and analyzed the sample agreements, you should be able to identify the issues to be addressed by your partnership agreement or incorporation documents, prepare your own outline for submission to your attorney, and more actively participate in final discussions with counsel. In addition to possibly reducing legal fees through your involvement in this process, you can take comfort in the thought that you have taken that crucial first step toward protecting the value of your practice and ensuring its effective management and continued success.

# Acknowledgments

The Management of an Accounting Practice Committee expresses its appreciation to the author of this book, Mark F. Murray of the Industry and Practice Management Division of the AICPA.

Members of the Management of an Accounting Practice Committee Task Force who provided direction, information, and reviews of the book are:

W. Thomas Cooper, CPA
Task Force Chairman
Potter and Company
Louisville, Kentucky

W. M. (Mack) Lawhon, CPA
Weaver and Tidwell
Fort Worth, Texas

James R. Beers, CPA
Beers and Cutler
Washington, DC

J. Stephen Moss, CPA
Urbach, Kahn & Werlin, P.C.
Burlington, Vermont

M. Dan Howard, CPA
Howard, Cunningham &
  Houchin
Lubbock, Texas

Raymond F. Murphy, Jr., CPA
Murphy & Company
Providence, Rhode Island

John M. Hughes, Jr., CPA
Levine, Hughes
  & Mithuen, Inc.
Englewood, Colorado

David E. Schlotzhauer, CPA
Mills & Schlotzhauer
Overland Park, Kansas

The Management of an Accounting Practice Committee gratefully recognizes attorney Paul E. Rumler of Denver, Colorado, for contributing his expertise in business organizations.

The Committee would also like to acknowledge the editorial efforts of Dan Deitz and Carrie Vaccaro; the production work of Ingrid Anderson, Robert DiCorcia, and Jeanmarie Brusati; and the guidance of Katharine Coveleski throughout the publication process.

# INTRODUCTION: HISTORICAL OVERVIEW

## PARTNERSHIPS

Traceable to the very origins of cooperative activity, the partnership is one of the oldest forms of business organization. Its roots extend from the sharecropping arrangements of ancient Babylon, Greece, and Rome to the shipping and trading enterprises of the fifteenth and sixteenth centuries. Today's partnerships are generally understood to be continuing relationships between two or more partners for purposes of conducting a business or carrying out a specific function. General partners share in profits, losses, and risks.

The traditional partnership is a small, egalitarian venture in which the partners participate actively in the management of the business and share profits and responsibilities equally. While this description applies to some partnerships, in many other cases one partner, or a particular group of partners, may rise within the organization, gaining greater responsibility and prestige than others do. On the other hand, some larger partnerships were never intended to be egalitarian entities. Their hierarchical characteristics stand in sharp contrast to those of the organizations from which they are descended. Regardless of their form, partnerships have always been, and will continue to be, an integral part of our economic and social systems. Indeed, it is a rarity to find a society in which partnership principles are not represented in its professional organizations.

Of all business relationships, the partnership is perhaps the most intimate and personal. By its very nature, a partnership's success is dependent upon mutual trust, confidence, and shared vision, thereby rendering those involved in the enterprise members of a business family, which is why a partnership is frequently compared to a marriage. As is the case in a marriage, a partnership's success is best assured if those involved remain committed not only to each other, but to the partnership itself. Often a minor deviation from the partnership plan can result in substantial damage to even the strongest of partnerships. Accordingly, the parties can maintain their professional direction and properly prepare for growth, change, and adversity through a partnership agreement.

Despite its long heritage, partnership law has evolved little since the general acceptance of the Uniform Partnership Act, which was approved in 1914 and which defines the partner relationship and provides a statutory scheme for resolving conflicts. Indeed, partnership law has become something of a sacred cow, with legal scholars and other commentators directing much of their attention instead to the well-publicized corporate issues of insider trading and hostile takeovers. However, this trend does not indicate that partnership activity is without economic or social consequence. On the contrary, millions of people have chosen this form of business organization, thereby affecting a substantial segment of this country's professional workforce and having a significant economic impact. As it relates to public accounting, the partnership continues to be an ideal way to conduct a practice, since it combines the range of resources available in the corporate structure with the responsibility, accountability, and personal service characteristics unique to sole proprietorships.

# PROFESSIONAL CORPORATIONS

Historically, the practice of public accounting has been conducted under the sole-proprietorship or partnership forms of practice. The trend toward practicing accounting as a professional corporation began in the 1970s, and the number of accounting practices being incorporated continues to grow. The main reasons for this movement in the profession are limited liability and inequities in the income tax status of fringe benefits for partnerships and corporations.

Although the IRS recognizes, and all states allow, the incorporation of accounting practices, this situation has not always been the case, and the number of incorporated practices varies among states. To overcome various inequities, specifically with respect to fringe benefits, professional groups first sought recognition as associations taxable as corporations; however, they encountered strong resistance. It was not until the landmark case of *United States v. Kintner*, decided in 1954, that the Court held that an unincorporated association that more closely resembled a corporation than a partnership should be taxed as a corporation. In 1959, the Treasury Department proposed revised regulations for determining when a particular business entity would be considered corporate in nature and would therefore be entitled to the attendant income tax benefits.

These regulations came to be known as the Kintner Regulations, and although they recognized the corporate treatment of unincorporated organizations, they were clearly intended to upset the Court's decision. Bestowing preferential treatment on some groups, such as theatrical and real estate organizations, the Kintner Regulations were so strict in their treatment of professionals that in a majority of states, professionals were unable to achieve corporate tax status. Professional groups responded by initiating legislation that provided for a special corporate structure for professional practices, and this legislation, which satisfied the Kintner Regulations, was adopted on a state-by-state basis.

The IRS was aware of the states' professional corporation statutes and recognized their intent to circumvent the Kintner Regulations. In 1965, the IRS amended the Kintner Regulations and created a corporate resemblance test that imposed a tremendous amount of corporate resemblance on affected organizations, overly stressed the technicalities of local statutes, and contradicted *Kintner* by denying corporate status to an organization situated in a state where the Uniform Partnership Act was in effect. For the remainder of the decade, the Treasury Department maintained its position that a professional organization was not a legitimate corporation, prompting decisive action by professionals. In a succession of lawsuits against the IRS, courts throughout the country held that the Kintner Regulations, as defined by the IRS in 1965, were arbitrary, discriminatory, and invalid. By 1969, the IRS conceded that professional organizations, structured and operated under state corporation acts, warranted classification as valid corporations and should be entitled to corporate income tax treatment. State, national, and professional organizations quickly followed suit and revised their codes of professional conduct. This debate finally ran its course by 1977, when the IRS revoked the 1965 amendments to the Kintner Regulations, which no longer influenced the tax classification of professional organizations.

# Table of Contents

# I
# PARTNERSHIP OR PROFESSIONAL CORPORATION?

All accounting firms strive to be profitable enterprises that provide top-quality services. The best way to attain this goal is to establish and maintain a well-planned, properly structured firm that meets the needs of your clients and staff. To achieve this type of practice, you need to select the business structure that will maximize profits and be consistent with your practice philosophy. Among the accountants' choices for practice organization are partnerships and professional corporations. The importance of your choice cannot be overstated, since the characteristics of your business structure can either impede or promote effective management and your firm's ability to achieve its goals.

To decide which form of practice is best for your firm, you need to consider those issues that are unique to your firm, such as service mix, staff expertise, size of practice, and client base, to name a few. However, it is beyond the scope of this book to address these aspects of planning your firm's structure. Instead, this book functions solely as an aid to drafting organizational documents.

Before you begin this task, solicit the personal and professional objectives of each member of your present or proposed firm. Reach a consensus on the philosophy of practice from which these objectives flow before you attempt to draft your agreements. Although scrutinizing your firm's policies, goals, and personnel in this manner may be time consuming, it will provide an ideal opportunity for a complete reassessment of all aspects of the firm. Problems that may have lingered unresolved can be reexamined in a new light and properly addressed.

You also need to study projections of the financial impact of the proposed structure on your practice and its individual partners and shareholders. You must weigh the advantages and disadvantages of each form of practice and of the various provisions contained in your agreements.

Decisions on practice organization require more than knowledge of the internal dynamics of your practice; they entail a thorough understanding of relevant tax and legal concepts, as well as jurisdictional law. Moreover, regulations, tax laws, and court decisions are constantly evolving. For this reason, the involvement of legal counsel is mandatory. When retaining an attorney, select one who specializes in business organizations, preferably those of accountants, so that your practice can receive the benefits of the expertise that it not only requires but also deserves.

The following chart, though not all-inclusive, illustrates the manner in which principal factors are treated when partnerships and professional corporations exist in their natural form. Bear in mind that laws may differ among states and that the treatment of some factors may be affected by personal management styles, philosophy of practice, and agreements among the parties.

# COMPARISON OF PARTNERSHIPS AND PROFESSIONAL CORPORATIONS

| Factors | General Partnership | Professional Corporation |
|---|---|---|
| Instrument of Creation | • No documents are required. Creation is achieved with the partners' *intent* to function as a partnership and to share the common purposes and risks of the enterprise on a consensual and ongoing basis. | • Articles and Certificate of Incorporation are required. |
| Organizational Documents | • Partnership Agreement. | • Articles of Incorporation.<br>• Bylaws.<br>• Employment Contract.<br>• Buy-Sell/Shareholders' Agreement.<br>• Corporate minutes. |
| Filing Requirements, Creation Costs, and Maintenance | • No state filing is required, although some states require the registration of the business name and registration with the State Board of Accountancy.<br><br>• File annual returns of income.<br><br>• Practicing without a written Partnership Agreement results in no creation costs.<br><br>• Practicing with a written Partnership Agreement results in costs being incurred in the drafting and updating of the agreement. | • File Articles of Incorporation with the appropriate state agency and annual or biannual corporate reports.<br><br>• File annual corporate income tax returns<br><br>• Purchase corporate materials: stock certificates, stock register, minute book, and corporate seal.<br><br>• More extensive legal services are usually required, and greater legal expenses are usually incurred through incorporating. |

*(continued)*

3

# COMPARISON OF PARTNERSHIPS AND PROFESSIONAL CORPORATIONS (cont.)

| Factors | General Partnership | Professional Corporation |
|---|---|---|
| Filing Requirements, Creation Costs, and Maintenance (cont.) | • Most expenses incurred for drafting and updating the agreement are tax-deductible or amortizable over 60 months. | • Legal expenses for establishing and monitoring a professional corporation are generally tax deductible or amortizable over 60 months.<br>• Draft and maintain organizational documents and employee benefit plans.<br>• Pay taxes: Social Security and Unemployment. |
| Liability | • Each partner is jointly and severally liable for the debts, obligations, and wrongful acts committed in the course of partnership business and for the misappropriation of property owned by third persons.<br><br>• If necessary, the assets of the partnership or partners can be attached. This rule applies regardless of the extent of the partner's interest in the partnership or involvement in the transaction from which the liability arose.<br><br>• While the extensive use of liability insurance has alleviated this situation to a great extent, liability remains a primary reason for accountants' incorporating their practices. | • Corporation is liable to the extent of its assets for all claims of creditors, including claims for negligence of its employees.<br><br>• Shareholders are not personally liable for the acts, contracts, or obligations of the corporation, its employees, or agents. However, personal liability attaches to the shareholder for the professional work that the shareholder personally performs or supervises.<br>• Insurance coverage is available; however, premiums may be higher than those charged to partnerships. |

| | |
|---|---|
| Transfer of Ownership | • Consent of other partners is usually required before transferring a partnership interest. <br><br> • Transfer of a 50% or greater partnership interest will terminate the partnership. | • Shares of stock enable a quicker, less complex transfer of ownership; however, transfer is still restricted to those qualified to practice accounting or by any terms in a shareholders' agreement. <br><br> • Transfer of a 50% or greater shareholders' interest will not necessarily terminate the corporation. |
| Continuity of Life | • The continuing existence of the partnership is subject to the partners' consensus. When they no longer hold themselves out to the public as a partnership, when one or more partners withdraw, die, or are not replaced by mutual and unanimous consent of the remaining partners, or when the partners breach their duties to other partners, the partnership may technically dissolve. Some states require new registration with the secretary of state if any of these events occur. <br><br> • Unless expressly limited, the duration of the partnership's business existence is at the will of the partners; therefore, partners have more control over dissolution of a partnership than a shareholder has over the dissolution of the corporation. | • The accounting practice continues beyond the professional life of any one shareholder. As a separate, legal entity, the corporation's existence is indefinite and continues beyond the withdrawal, death, expulsion, or bankruptcy of a shareholder or upon the sale of stock, unless dissolved by voluntary proceedings attributable to some event, such as bankruptcy or failure to adhere to state regulatory requirements. |

*(continued)*

5

# COMPARISON OF PARTNERSHIPS AND PROFESSIONAL CORPORATIONS (cont.)

| *Factors* | *General Partnership* | *Professional Corporation* |
|---|---|---|
| Dissolvability | • Freely dissolvable with no filing requirements.<br><br>• Dissolution can occur through the express will of the partners; withdrawal, death, disability, or expulsion of a partner; bankruptcy of the partnership; or judicial decree. | • Required to make filings with the appropriate state agency, usually the secretary of state, to achieve dissolution.<br><br>• A corporation is generally unaffected by the condition of a shareholder.<br><br>• Tax issues are more complex when dissolving a professional corporation. |
| Management | • Authority is at times not centralized but is, rather, divided among partners, with each having an equal right to participate in the management of the partnership. Some partnerships may centralize authority in a managing partner or committee. | • Authority is centralized, with management functions vested in a Board of Directors elected annually by shareholders. Directors elect the officers who conduct the affairs of the corporation. |
| Benefits | • Group term life insurance is available (not deductible).<br><br>• Partners cannot benefit from medical reimbursement plan.<br><br>• Partners can deduct only 25% of health insurance premiums. | • Group term life insurance is available (not deductible).<br><br>• Medical reimbursement plans are available.<br><br>• Health and accident insurance is available. |

|  | |
|---|---|
|  | • Wage continuation plans are available.<br>• Disability insurance, premium payments, or reimbursements are available.<br><br>• Retirement plans are comparable to corporate-sponsored plans. |
| Taxes | • Income tax is imposed at partner level; however, this is not always true at the state level.<br><br>• Tax issues for partnership are more complex than they are for professional corporations in situations other than dissolution. | • Possibly, two levels of income tax are imposed:<br>  1. One at the corporate level.<br>  2. One at the shareholder level for distributions made by the corporation.<br><br>*Note that one level of income tax can be achieved through an S corporation election.*<br><br>• Possible double taxation upon liquidation. |

# II
# PARTNERSHIP
# AGREEMENTS

## BACKGROUND

Through an enforceable partnership agreement, partners are able to define their own relationship. However, in the absence of a written agreement, state law determines the rights and obligations of the partners. More than a typical contract between unaffiliated parties, a partnership agreement is fundamental to an efficient, profitable practice. It governs partner relations and sets forth their rights, responsibilities, and obligations. Composed of clear, specific, and unambiguous language that accurately reflects the partners' intentions, your agreement should be detailed enough to address all necessary issues yet sufficiently flexible to accommodate changing circumstances, particularly with respect to firm growth and expanded services. Of course, even the most comprehensive agreement cannot address every conceivable situation or change in circumstance, but it certainly should address foreseeable problems and provide some guidelines to resolve unforeseeable ones. As a practical, workable document, your partnership agreement should be readily understood by all partners and should not require regular interpretation from legal counsel. When properly prepared, your agreement can result in a professional relationship that yields both collective and individual benefits.

## THE INITIAL STEP

A question commonly posed by practitioners concerns the appropriate time when a partnership agreement should be prepared. The answer is that it is never too early to begin your agreement. Have your agreement drafted as soon as possible and before you and your partners become personally committed to management practices or concepts on which you may not agree. Such disagreements frequently arise because of a lack of shared understanding of what is expected from all partners in the firm, making it difficult, if not impossible, to reach a consensus.

Your first step is to determine the professional and personal needs of the members of your business family, since these needs play an integral role in the drafting of your agreement. This task can be made less burdensome if you and your partners are sensitive to each other's opinions and institute and maintain effective channels of communication. Your agreement should be consistent with your firm's philosophy yet recognize the differing expectations of the partners. Failure to create such an agreement may invite conflict and, for some partners, may lower not only the quality of life, but also productivity.

## AN OVERLOOKED NECESSITY

Although some partnerships appear to function adequately without a written agreement, generally it is in spite of, rather than because of, this omission. Other firms may be practicing under agreements that have not been ratified by all partners, are outdated, or are oral in form. Accountants are not alone in this predicament. Other professionals, particularly in the fields of law and medicine, often conduct their practices in a similar fashion.

There are several reasons for this situation. Partners in accounting firms are so involved in responding to client needs that they fail to properly plan their own future. Further, the process of writing a partnership agreement may raise some psychological barriers. For example, partners may anticipate the short-term negative fall-out and conflicts that are likely to arise when each partner's true values and expectations are revealed, thereby deteriorating the partnership relationship. However, far greater deterioration may ultimately occur if issues vital to the management of your practice remain unresolved. Long-standing conflicts do not vanish; rather, they fester and ultimately emerge. Additionally, partners may be reluctant to address such complex and unpleasant issues as disability, death, withdrawal, or expulsion.

Another barrier, one that affects not only accountants but other professionals as well, is resistance to formalities, particularly, resistance to the formalities of a written partnership agreement. Resistance is frequently due to a partner's false sense of security with an unwritten agreement, reliance on precedent, or, in the case of a younger partner, a desire to keep one's professional options open. In addition, many accountants practice under the misconception that as long as the firm remains profitable and efficient, any problems that may exist will resolve themselves.

The reluctance of partners to practice under a partnership agreement exists not only in firms that have operated for a number of years but also in firms that have just begun. When creating their business relationship, partners typically can foresee only professional success and personal satisfaction; therefore, they can easily overlook this exercise. This condition is further exacerbated by the ease with which partnerships can be created and the discretionary nature of organizational documents. Unlike professional corporations, partnerships may be organized without complying with any formalities. Attorneys may not be consulted, and documents may not be drafted. In some instances, accounting partnerships originate with nothing more than a handshake between partners. In others, practitioners merely attach clauses to a preprinted form or provide their attorney with vague details concerning their professional and personal goals.

Unfortunately, the harsh reality of practicing without a partnership agreement or under a deficient agreement appears too late—when a partner is permanently disabled, dies, or is expelled. In addition to gross inequities in compensation, the usual consequences are resentment, serious disputes, loss of clients, litigation, legal expenses, and the possible dissolution of the firm. These consequences may be avoided through a timely, skillfully drafted partnership agreement.

## OBJECTIVES

Considering the effort involved in changing personal and business methods and the time devoted by most accountants to their practices, it is not surprising that some practitioners function without partnership agreements. However, once you realize the value of charting your professional future and overcome obstacles, the result will be worth the effort.

The benefits that result from a partnership agreement are as unique and individual as your firm. The chart below illustrates some of the most prominent objectives of a partnership agreement and identifies the provisions through which they are achieved.

### OBJECTIVES OF A PARTNERSHIP AGREEMENT

| *Objective* | *Applicable Provisions* |
| --- | --- |
| To guard against the unpredictable, thereby protecting your investment, livelihood, and the most valuable asset in your estate | • Disability<br>• Death<br>• Retirement<br>• Resignation<br>• Expulsion<br>• Insurance<br>• Dissolution/Liquidation<br>• Methods used to resolve disputes<br>• Involuntary transfers |
| To state, in a formal way, what is expected of each partner | • Capital contributions<br>• Time devoted to practice<br>• Noncompetition Agreements<br>• Rights to firm clients and property |

| *Objective* | *Applicable Provisions* |
|---|---|
| | • Restrictions on transfer of ownership<br>• Filing of tax returns<br>• Partners' role in the management of the firm<br>• Partnership meetings<br>• Duties of managing partner |
| To inform each partner of financial returns and responsibilities to the partnership | • Compensation<br>• Profit/Loss allocation<br>• Payments upon retirement<br>• Capital contributions<br>• Right to draw upon capital account<br>• Loans and contracting among partners and other employees<br>• Treatment of expenses<br>• Determination of new partner's ownership<br>• Nonequity versus equity partners<br>• Restrictions on the transfer of partnership interest<br>• Vacation allotments<br>• Filing tax returns |
| To direct a partner's career path | • Compensation<br>• Admission of new partners<br>• Determination of new partnership ownership<br>• Nonequity partner becoming equity partner |
| To provide for an orderly separation from, or dissolution of, the partnership | • Disposition of assets and liabilities<br>• Continuing operation of the firm/winding up<br>• Distribution of partnership proceeds and files<br>• Events that bring about dissolution |

*(continued)*

**OBJECTIVES OF A PARTNERSHIP AGREEMENT (cont.)**

| *Objective* | *Applicable Provisions* |
|---|---|
| To provide for an orderly separation from, or dissolution of, the partnership (cont.) | • Partner's position in the surviving firm in the case of sale or merger<br>• Continuation of insurance<br>• Consequences of partner disability, death, retirement, resignation, or expulsion<br>• Methods used to resolve disputes |

In addition to these objectives, practicing under a partnership agreement promotes teamwork and the appreciation of partners' efforts by other partners, thereby increasing productivity and the quality of life. The practitioner also experiences peace of mind, knowing that order has been imposed on those practice issues that can be controlled. Even the most skillfully drafted agreement may not resolve all existing and potential conflicts, but it should provide a method for resolving disputes and foster acceptance of those conditions that cannot be changed.

# PERIODIC REEXAMINATION

Accounting partnerships are long-term, dynamic entities that are constantly evolving. Your partnership agreement must be periodically reviewed and adapted to the changing financial and personal needs of the partners and the partnership. It is vital that partners monitor the direction of the firm on an ongoing basis so that existing and potential problems can be identified and resolved.

Regular examination of, and necessary modifications to, your partnership agreement will enable your accounting practice to continue to prosper. There is no universal rule that determines the time and frequency of reviewing a partnership agreement; this depends upon a firm's own particular needs and practice philosophy. However, one approach taken by many firms is to phrase the agreement provisions so that they are able to accommodate changes in firm circumstances without requiring a revision of the entire agreement. A practice that operates along these lines results in a more practical agreement and in a saving of partners' time.

# SAMPLE ACCOUNTING FIRM PARTNERSHIP AGREEMENT

*CAVEAT: The following 122 provisions cover issues that should be considered when drafting a partnership agreement. The selected provisions, each of which serves as one suggested approach to addressing a particular issue, may be phrased and arranged in your own agreement in a manner different from that used in this sample. Since the choice of provisions depends on a firm's goals and management style, it may not be necessary to include every provision contained in the sample agreement. Accordingly, this agreement functions as a pool of provisions from which partners can choose, and it can be modified to conform to the individual needs of your practice. Keep in mind that your partnership agreement must be prepared by your attorney and that it must comply with prevailing tax laws, regulations, and statutory law.*

## Partnership Agreement

AGREEMENT made this _____ day of _____ 19xx, among Joseph F. Delong of [*city, state*], Anton E. Wagner of [*city, state*], Martha A. Bonner of [*city, state*], Dorothy M. Convery of [*city, state*], and R. Blane Holmes of [*city, state*] pursuant to the provisions of the [*governing state*] Uniform Partnership Act.

WHEREAS, all of the parties to this Agreement are licensed to practice public accounting in the state of _____; and

WHEREAS, the parties desire to form a Partnership for the practice of public accountancy;

THEREFORE, IT IS MUTUALLY AGREED AS FOLLOWS:

# ARTICLE I

## ORGANIZATION

1.1 **Name of Partnership:** The name of the Partnership shall be [*name of Partnership*] and all Partnership business shall be

*FOR DISCUSSION PURPOSES ONLY*

conducted in such name. All Partnership property shall be held in the name of the Partnership and not in the name of any Partner. If for any reason any person whose name is included in the Partnership's name ceases to be a Partner, the remaining Partners may, in their discretion, delete the former Partner's name or continue to use such name free of compensation.

The use of said individual Partner's name as provided above is subject to, and conditioned upon, the Partnership being, and continuing to be, in good standing in the profession of public accounting, and if such is not the case, the Partnership shall have no further right or claim to the continued use of said Partner's name thereafter.

1.2    **Organization:**   The Partnership is hereby organized as a [*governing state*] general partnership. The Partners shall make all filings and disclosures required by, and shall otherwise comply with, the applicable laws of the State of [*governing state*].

1.3    **Term:**   The Partnership shall begin on the effective date of this document and shall continue until terminated as herein provided or by operation of law. The disability, death, retirement, withdrawal, termination, or bankruptcy of any Partner shall not dissolve or terminate the Partnership.

1.4    **Place of Business:**   The principal place of Partnership business shall be located at [*address*]. The Partnership shall be entitled to establish other Partnership offices both within and without [*state*] and to change the principal office as may be approved by a majority of the Partners.

All Partners shall execute the lease of all business premises and agree to share equally in all related rents, costs, losses, income, and expenses in accordance with the profit allocation formula.

1.5    **Purposes:**   The purpose of the Partnership is to engage in the general practice of accounting, carry on related activities, and manage any property which comes to the Partnership by way of fees or investments so long as such activity is consistent with the laws of [*governing state*] or the rules, regulations, and ethical standards of the State Board of Accountancy, the American Institute of Certified Public Accountants, and the [*governing state*] Society of Certified Public Accountants.

1.6 **Purposes Restricted:** The Partnership shall function as a Partnership only for the purpose specified in Section 1.5 hereof. The Partnership is prohibited from engaging in any other activity or business, and Partners shall have no authority to hold themselves out as general agents of another Partner in any other activity.

1.7 **No Payments of Individual Obligations:** The Partnership's assets and credit shall be used by the Partners solely for the benefit of the Partnership. The Partnership's assets shall not be transferred or used in any way for the payment of any individual Partner obligation.

1.8 **Title to Property:** The Partnership shall own, as an entity, all real and personal property, and Partners shall have no ownership interest in such property in their individual names or rights. Each Partner's Partnership interest shall be personal property for all purposes.

# ARTICLE II

## DEFINITIONS

*It is customary to include, at the beginning of an Agreement, the definition of frequently recurring terms. Although the particular terms identified and defined by each firm will differ, the list below contains some suggested definitions.*

- ''Act'' shall mean the [*governing state*] Uniform Partnership Act as now in effect or as hereafter amended.
- ''Agreement'' shall mean this Agreement of Partnership as the same may be amended or supplemented from time to time.

*FOR DISCUSSION PURPOSES ONLY*

Words such as "hereof," "herein," and "hereto" refer to this Agreement as a whole, unless the context requires otherwise. The term "provisions of this Agreement" includes the terms and provisions hereof and of all such amendments.

- "Capital Contributions" shall mean the amount of money contributed by each Partner to the Partnership with respect to the Partnership Interest held by such Partner pursuant to the terms of this Agreement.

- "Estate" shall mean the estate or any successor in interest of a Partner, Retiree, or Disabled Partner, so long as any payments are due to or from such estate or successor in interest, under any provisions in this Agreement.

- "Executive Committee" shall mean the committee composed of not less than three (3) or more than five (5) Partners chosen by the Partnership to assume the duties set forth in Section 7.4.

- "Expulsion" shall mean action by the Partnership effecting termination of a Partner's interest in the Partnership.

- "Firm" or "Partnership," interchangeable terms in this document, shall include the firm now organized and the same continuing firm, however named, notwithstanding changes in personnel by additions of new Partners or termination of the membership of any Partners.

- "Managing Partner" shall mean the person elected to the office of Managing Partner in accordance with Section 7.1.

- "Partners" shall include, unless expressly qualified, all Partners individually whose membership has not been terminated.

- "Permanent Disability of a Partner" shall mean that disability which justifies the requisite vote of the Partners in their discretion to terminate, on that account, all his interest in the Partnership.

- "Percentage of Interest" shall mean, with respect to each Partner, his percentage of ownership in the Partnership and the corresponding assets and avails therefore. This interest may vary from time to time. Each Partner's percentage of Partnership Interest in the Partnership shall be based on his relative capital contributions to the Partnership.

- "Retired Partner" shall mean one whose participation in the voting of Partners and in the sharing of profits and losses is suspended, but who is eligible to receive retirement payments in accordance with the terms of this document.

*FOR DISCUSSION PURPOSES ONLY*

# ARTICLE III

## PARTNER'S FINANCIAL INTEREST

3.1 **Capital Contributions:**  The capital of the Partnership shall be maintained at a sufficient level as to adequately provide necessary working capital and facilities for the operation of the business, as determined by the Executive Committee. A Partner's capital contribution shall be _____ percent (____%) of the average of the Partner's salary for the current year and the immediately preceding _____ (____) years. The initial capital contribution shall be made in cash concurrently with the execution of this Agreement and maintained in a capital account for each Partner. The names, addresses, and initial capital contributions of each Partner are set forth below, and they shall be revised from time to time to reflect the admission and withdrawal of Partners.

> Joseph F. Delong          $x
> 68 Fetherston Avenue
> City, State
>
> Anton E. Wagner          $x
> 23 Holland Avenue
> City, State
>
> Martha A. Bonner          $x
> 4402 Mentone Street
> City, State
>
> Dorothy M. Convery          $x
> 210½ Wilder Street
> City, State
>
> R. Blane Holmes          $x
> 86 Columbia Avenue
> City, State

*(This information may be included in an attached schedule.)*

3.2 **Capital Accounts:**  Separate capital accounts shall be maintained by the Partnership for each Partner. The capital account of each Partner shall be credited with his capital contribution and shall be appropriately adjusted to reflect each Partner's allocation of profits, losses, and distributions.

3.3     **Interest:**   No interest shall be paid to Partners on any contributions to capital.

3.4     **Additional Capital Contributions:**   Partners shall make capital contributions in excess of the amounts set forth in Section 3.1 whenever they determine that such capital contributions are necessary or desirable to accomplish the Partnership's objectives. A Partner's failure to make the requisite additional capital contribution within _____ (____) days of the determination by the Partners that additional capital is necessary will result in that Partner's being held in breach of this provision.

This provision shall apply only to current Partners.

3.5     **Profits and Losses:**   The net profits and losses of the Partnership shall be divided or borne as set out by agreements among the Partners, except that all losses resulting from the wrongful act, dishonesty, or gross negligence of any Partner shall be charged to him in full before any allocation is made of other Partners' net earnings.

To the extent that the loss attributable to Partner misconduct is greater than the offending Partner's capital account, the loss shall be charged against his interest in future profits.

The basis of participation by Partners in profits and losses may be altered, as of _____ in any year, by unanimous agreement of the Partners.

3.6     **Priority and Distribution of Assets:**   Except as otherwise provided herein, no Partner shall have priority over any other Partner either as to the return of capital or as to profits, losses, or distributions. No Partner shall have the right to demand or receive property other than cash for his capital in the Partnership or in payment of his share of profits or cash flow.

3.7     **Drawings from Capital Account:**   Drawings exceeding salaries shall be made only with a two-thirds (⅔) vote of the Partners.

3.8   **Loans to the Partnership:**   In addition to making the mandatory capital contributions discussed herein, the Partners may be required by the Managing Partner to loan the Partnership additional capital on a pro rata basis. This amount will be in proportion to each Partner's ownership in the firm. The interest on additional capital loans will be treated as a Partnership expense and not as an income-distribution adjustment.

# ARTICLE IV

## COMPENSATION

4.1   **Partners' Salaries:**   Each Partner shall be compensated for services rendered to the Partnership. The Partnership shall deduct such salaries as a necessary expense of business before determining net profits.

Any Partner's salary may be increased or reduced at any time by unanimous agreement of the Partners. For the fiscal year ending _____, 19xx, the Partners' salaries are:

| | |
|---|---|
| Joseph F. Delong | $x |
| Anton E. Wagner | $x |
| Martha A. Bonner | $x |
| Dorothy M. Convery | $x |
| R. Blane Holmes | $x |

*(This information may be included in an attached schedule.)*

4.2   **Drawing Account:**   A drawing account, over and above salaries, shall be maintained for each Partner from which he shall have the right to draw against anticipated earnings, in monthly installments, an amount not exceeding _____ percent (____%) of his earnings for the preceding year. However, in no event shall a Partner's withdrawals exceed his proportionate share of Partnership profits. Any Partner shall have the right, at the end of any calendar year, to withdraw the balance of his share of the Partnership profits for that year. The drawings

*FOR DISCUSSION PURPOSES ONLY*

of Partners during the first year of the Partnership shall not exceed the following:

| | |
|---|---|
| Joseph F. Delong | $x |
| Anton E. Wagner | $x |
| Martha A. Bonner | $x |
| Dorothy M. Convery | $x |
| R. Blane Holmes | $x |

*[This information may be included in an attached schedule.]*

Withdrawals shall be charged against the Partner's distributive share of Partnership profits.

# ARTICLE V
## BENEFITS

5.1    **Vacations:**  Each Partner shall be entitled to an annual vacation of _____ (____) weeks during the first three (3) years of employment and _____ (____) weeks during the fourth (4th) year and thereafter, without loss of compensation. The times for such vacation periods shall be those most convenient to the Partnership.

5.2    **Sick Leave:**  Each Partner shall be entitled to annual sick leave of _____ (____) weeks because of sickness or accident to the Partner or any member of the Partner's immediate family. The Partner shall receive his full salary and share of profits. Sick leave remaining from one (1) year may not be used in a future year or used for additional vacation.

Each Partner who becomes pregnant shall be entitled to _____ (____) weeks' maternity leave.

*Editor's Note: It may be appropriate to address parental leave in this article.*

5.3    **Vacations and Leaves Exceeding Limits:**  If any Partner's vacation, sick leave, maternity leave, or parental leave exceeds the specified yearly limits, such Partner's weekly salary shall be reduced by _____ percent (____%) for each week of vacation, sick leave, maternity leave, or parental leave that exceeds the specified yearly limits.

5.4 **Leaves of Absence:** Any Partner may obtain a leave of absence from the Partnership for such reasons, during such periods, and subject to such conditions as the Managing Partner shall provide. Any such agreement which extends beyond a one- (1-) year period shall be subject to the approval of a majority vote of the Partners other than the affected Partner.

5.5 **Professional Development:** In addition to vacation, sick leave, maternity leave, and parental leave, each Partner shall be entitled to _____ (____) days in each fiscal year to attend professional meetings and continuing education.

5.6 **Professional Liability Insurance:** The Partnership shall have in force for each Partner, professional liability insurance. The minimum coverage for each policy shall be _____ dollars ($____) per incident or, if the maximum coverage under the American Institute of Certified Public Accountants' plan is less, then such lesser amount.

5.7 **Continuing Insurance:** The Partnership shall continue to insure each retiring Partner under its malpractice insurance policy for a minimum of _____ (____) years following full retirement. Insurance coverage beyond this period shall be within the Partnership's discretion.

5.8 **Life Insurance:** The Managing Partner, in his discretion, shall determine, from time to time, what life insurance, if any, shall be carried on the lives of Partners for the benefit of the firm.

# ARTICLE VI

## CHANGES IN OWNERSHIP

6.1 **Admission of New Partners:** At any time during the Partnership's fiscal year, a new Partner may be admitted to the

Partnership; however, a two-thirds (⅔) vote of all Partners is required. Each new Partner must be in good standing and not be legally prohibited from becoming a partner in a partnership organized for the practice of accounting under the laws of [*governing state*]. Each new Partner shall be required to execute this Agreement and all supplements to it. The Partnership shall not dissolve upon the admission of a new Partner.

6.2 **New Partner's Ownership:** Once admitted to the Partnership, each Partner shall be allowed to purchase an equity amount agreed to by the Partners. This amount is set forth in Schedule A attached hereto.

6.3 **No Classes of Partners:** Though their contractual rights differ, as provided by this Agreement, all Partners are of the same class and have identical and equal rights, except as otherwise provided herein.

6.4 **Sale or Merger:** If a Partner has not acquired his entire equity interest when a sale or merger of the Partnership or its assets occurs, then that Partner may accelerate his buy-in and receive the percentage of gain that is equal to the equity interest that he has acquired at the accelerated level. However, he shall not receive that percentage of the gain on the equity interest that he has not acquired.

6.5 **Waiver of Partition:** No Partner shall take any action resulting in the partition or appraisement of the Partnership or any of its assets or cause the sale of any Partnership property, and notwithstanding any provisions of this Agreement or applicable law to the contrary, each Partner irrevocably waives any right to institute and maintain any action for partition or to necessitate any sale of his Partnership interest, or any Partnership assets, except as provided herein.

6.6 **Non-Equity Partner:** A non-equity Partner shall not receive any interest in the Partnership's capital or equity; rather, his interest shall be limited to the Partnership's net profits and losses, and his interest in the Partnership's income shall not be subject to buy-in. A non-equity Partner may become an equity Partner upon the unanimous vote of the equity Partners.

6.7 **Withdrawal:** A Partner may withdraw from the Partnership at any time upon delivery to the Managing Partner of sixty (60) days' prior written notice to all Partners specifying the date upon which such resignation is to become effective.

Such withdrawal shall not dissolve the Partnership, which shall continue among the remaining Partners.

6.8 **Payments to a Withdrawing Partner:** The withdrawing Partner shall be entitled to receive: (i) the amount of his capital account as of the end of the month withdrawal was effective, (ii) his proportional share of any fees received by the continuing Partnership subsequent to the end of the month for accounts receivable or work in process as of the end of the month, and (iii) the undrawn portion of his share of the Partnership profits, if any, as of the end of the month.

The withdrawing Partner shall be entitled to receive the Partnership interest in _____ (____) equal monthly installments beginning the month following the date of withdrawal. All payments, other than the return of capital, are intended to be taxable to the recipients as compensation for past services and deductible by the remaining Partners.

The remaining Partners shall have the right to deduct from the amount payable to the withdrawing Partner his proportionate share of any debts and/or reasonable reserve for liabilities not reflected on the Partnership books as of the end of the month.

If agreed upon by all of the parties in writing, any other method of payment may be utilized in compensating the withdrawing Partner for his interest in the Partnership.

6.9 **Bankruptcy or Insolvency of a Partner:** Should any Partner become bankrupt or insolvent, the other Partners shall have the right to deem such bankruptcy or insolvency as a withdrawal of the Partner and, upon written notification to such Partner, proceed with an accounting payment schedule as provided in Section 6.8.

6.10  **Partial Liquidation of a Partnership Interest:**  A Partner who wishes to dispose of part of his interest in the firm can do so only through other Partners in the firm. Each Partner has the right to purchase an interest equal to his proportionate percentage interest in the firm disregarding the interest of the selling Partner.

6.11  **Execution of Documents:**  Prior to the distribution described in Section 6.8, the withdrawing Partner shall execute such documents and take such action as shall be reasonably required by the Managing Partner to satisfy any obligations of the withdrawing Partner.

6.12  **Partial Disability:**  A Partner shall be considered partially disabled when a physician designated by the Partnership declares him unable to perform his professional responsibilities for more than _____ (____) hours per week for a period of more than _____ (____) months. Upon the partial disability of any partner who has been a Partner for more than _____ (____) years, the Partnership shall pay to the Partner, for _____ (____) years, beginning on the first day of partial disability, salary-continuation payments in equal monthly installments in an annual amount equal to the average of the compensation allocated to the Partner in the preceding _____ (____) years.

6.13  **Total Disability:**  A Partner shall be considered totally disabled when he becomes eligible to receive benefits under the Partnership's long-term disability insurance policy which is carried for the benefit of its employees.

Upon the total disability of any Partner, he shall receive salary-continuation payments equal to those calculated for partial disability during the first _____ (____) years of total disability; however, such amounts shall be reduced to the extent that their payment would eliminate or decrease any available disability insurance benefits.

*FOR DISCUSSION PURPOSES ONLY*

Should any Partner be continuously totally disabled for more than _____ (____) years, he shall be forthwith retired, and retirement procedures as provided for in Section 6.19 of this Agreement shall take effect.

6.14 **Expulsion for Cause:** A Partner shall be expelled for cause when it has been determined by a two-thirds (⅔) vote of Partners that any of the following reasons for his expulsion exist:

- Suspension or other major disciplinary action of any duly constituted authority
- Professional misconduct or violation of the code of professional ethics, if such misconduct continues after its desistance has been requested by the Managing Partner
- Action that injures the professional standing of the firm, if such action continues after its desistance is requested by the Managing Partner
- Insolvency, bankruptcy, or assignment of assets for the benefit of creditors, if such acts injure the professional standing of the firm
- Breach of any provision of this Agreement, which all other Partners expressly agree is a major provision, if, after the breach has been specified as a prospective ground for expulsion by written notice given by the Managing Partner, the same breach continues or occurs again

6.15 **Effects of Expulsion for Cause:** Upon a determination that a Partner be expelled for cause, he shall thereby be so expelled and shall have no right or interest thereafter in the firm or any of its assets, clientele, files, records, or affairs. He shall have thereafter no further professional duties to the firm or any of its clients and shall be privileged to serve none of them thereafter. He shall immediately remove himself and his personal effects from the firm offices. Upon any such expulsion, the expelled Partner shall be obligated not to accept engagements for professional services from any who have been clients of the firm during the last five (5) years preceding the determination of expulsion, the obligation not to accept such engagements being a continuing one for a term of the next ensuing five (5) years. This does not preclude

*FOR DISCUSSION PURPOSES ONLY*

full-time employment with a client. From the time of the expulsion, the expelled Partner shall have no participation whatever in the income or losses of the firm or any distribution or drawings from the net income. Realizing that the existence of any such cause for expulsion may bring disgrace on the firm and damage the firm in amounts and ways that cannot be calculated or become liquidated in amount, each Partner agrees that the firm shall succeed to all of the rights of the expelled Partner as hereinabove set forth and shall retain all sums unpaid by it to the expelled Partner, whether accrued or not at that time; further, that the receipt and retention by the firm of all such rights and sums shall satisfy and discharge the damages of the firm, being retained as and thereby determined to be liquidated damages, no other indebtedness of the expelled Partner to the firm being discharged.

6.16    **Separation Without Determining Any Cause Therefor:**    A Partner shall be separated immediately when, on the recommendation of the Managing Partner, it is determined by a two-thirds (⅔) vote of the Partners that he shall be separated without determination of any cause therefor. This method of separation may be employed notwithstanding the fact that grounds may exist for expulsion for cause.

6.17    **Effects of Separation Without Determining Any Cause Therefor:**    Upon such separation without determining a cause therefor, the Partner so separated shall have no right or interest thereafter in the firm nor shall he have any further professional duties to the firm. He shall immediately remove himself and his personal effects from the firm offices. Except as otherwise provided in this provision, a Partner so separated shall be entitled to the same rights, the same payments by, and be subject to the same duties to, the continuing firm as if he were then retiring from the firm under Section 6.19 or, if he continues in public practice, Section 6.8 shall apply.

6.18    **Retirement:**    A Partner may retire on not less than sixty (60) days' written notice at the end of the fiscal year during which he shall have attained the age of fifty-five (55). The retirement of a Partner shall be compulsory at the end of the fiscal year during which he shall have attained the age of sixty-five (65) years unless the continuation of his services is requested by a two-thirds (⅔) vote of the Partners. Upon retirement, a Partner shall be entitled to payments under Section 6.19 of this Agreement.

6.19 **Payments to Retired/Deceased Partners:** A retired or deceased Partner shall receive—

- The balance of his capital account as of the date of retirement/death, payable without interest within _____ (____) days of retirement/death.
- _____ percent (____%) of the average of the retired/ deceased Partner's taxable income from the firm during each of the last _____ (____) completed fiscal years of the firm during which he was a Partner, payable in _____ (____) equal [*annual, quarterly, or monthly*] installments, without interest, beginning _____ (____) days after retirement/death.
- His share of undistributed net income for the current year as of the end of the month in which retirement/death occurred. An adjustment shall be made to accrue normal and prepaid expenses other than those for stationery and supplies.

If the retiring or deceased Partner owes the Partnership any amount, on account of loans or distributions or for any other reason, such amounts shall be offset against the amounts payable to the retiring Partner or his estate, and if the Partnership has entered into any guarantee on his behalf, such guarantee shall be discharged before any payment is made to such retiring Partner or his estate, and in connection therewith, the Partnership shall have the right to apply any payments due such retiring or deceased Partner to the payment of the amount guaranteed. Any amounts owing to the Partnership, in excess of the amounts owing to such retiring or deceased Partner, shall become immediately due and payable on demand.

*FOR DISCUSSION PURPOSES ONLY*

All payments, other than the return of capital, shall be taxable to the retiring Partner or his estate as compensation for past services and be deductible by the remaining Partners.

If agreed upon by all of the parties in writing, any other method of payment may be utilized to compensate the retiring Partner or the deceased Partner's estate for his interest in the Partnership.

6.20 **Right to Examine Books:**  Any person legally entitled to receive payments under this Agreement shall be entitled to examine the Partnership's books, upon reasonable notice and at reasonable times, to the extent that such examination shall be necessary to determine the amount of payments due him.

6.21 **Retiring/Deceased Partners—Execution of Documents:** On the closing date, the Partnership and the retiring Partner or the representative/estate of deceased Partner or its representative shall execute documents and instruments of conveyance as may be necessary or appropriate to confirm the redemption of the retiring/deceased Partner's interest, the withdrawal of the retiring/deceased Partner as a Partner as of the date of the retiring event/death, and the assumption by the Partnership of all liabilities of the retiring/deceased Partner with respect to the Partnership.

6.22 **Partial Retirement:**  Prior to attaining the age of sixty (60), a Partner may request partial retirement. This request shall be granted upon the unanimous agreement of all Partners.

6.23 **Adjustment to Retirement Benefits:**  Should the Partnership Agreement liberalize the retirement provisions while payments are being made to a retired Partner, the Partnership shall apply the more liberal provisions to the unpaid portion of the retiree's benefits.

6.24 **Death While Retired:**  Should the retiring Partner die prior to receiving his full retirement benefits, any benefits due him shall be paid to his estate in the same manner as they would have been paid had he continued to live.

6.25 **Hold Harmless:**   The Partnership shall hold the retiring Partner harmless from all costs, liabilities, and expenses which occur after the Partner retires.

# ARTICLE VII

## GOVERNANCE

*Managing Partner*

7.1 **Managing Partner:**   The Managing Partner, from the effective date of this Agreement, shall be _____, and he shall be elected by a two-thirds (⅔) vote of the Partners for a term of _____ (____) year(s). On the Managing Partner's death, disability, or resignation, a successor Managing Partner shall be elected by a majority of the Partners. The Managing Partner may be removed by a two-thirds (⅔) vote of the other Partners, with each Partner having one (1) vote.

Any Partner who has attained the age of sixty (60) is no longer eligible to be the Managing Partner or hold any administrative position in the firm.

7.2 **Duties of Managing Partner:**   Subject to the express terms of this Agreement, which as to certain matters provides that firm decisions shall be determined by the Executive Committee or by a specific vote of the Partners, the complete and sole management of the firm is hereby vested in the Managing Partner. He shall consult with the non-managing Partners, but the final decision rests with him. His duties shall include—

• Managing Partnership's daily activities and administering firm policies, procedures, and long-range plans.
• Delegating both professional and administrative functions to other Partners, managers, and staff.

*FOR DISCUSSION PURPOSES ONLY*

- Organizing Partnership operations, developing departments and specialties, and maintaining performance standards.
- Developing quality control procedures.
- Defining criteria, pursuing acquisitions, and developing offices.
- Maintaining effective firm-wide objectives and organizational structure.
- Insuring adequate working conditions—space, equipment, supervision, and opportunity.
- Authorizing Partners to transact business with clients.
- Providing Partner and staff training in technical and managerial skills.
- Deciding to withhold Partner salaries or draws if a cash flow problem exists.
- Exercising financial controls to achieve firm goals, including: financial reporting, billing rate determination, budget management, account billing, and receivables control.
- Providing and maintaining adequate insurance coverage for all appropriate areas of firm concern.
- Maintaining the firm's profitability.
- Insuring adequate working capital by defining requirements, controlling capital withdrawals, maintaining borrowing lines, and coordinating purchasing.
- Entering contracts or purchasing assets up to _____ dollars ($____) per item.
- Committing to short-term loans on behalf of the Partnership.
- Preparing and adopting a schedule of professional fees for all Partners and staff.
- Investing Partnership funds at no risk.
- Authorizing and executing contracts, commitments, and other legal documents in a manner consistent with this Agreement.
- Directing all firm-related litigation.
- Sitting on committee boards, speaking at community functions, and participating in local civic organizations.
- Resolving disputes between Partners.
- Motivating staff to improve.
- Monitoring, administering, and, with the input of Partners, updating this Agreement.

- Keeping Partners informed of concerns by all appropriate means, including scheduling annual and special Partnership meetings.
- Designating those who shall execute contracts, agreements, or other instruments on the Partnership's behalf.

The Managing Partner may not—

- Independently admit or expel any Partner.
- Increase his own salary.
- Violate any provision of this Agreement.
- Invest Partnership funds in risky ventures.
- Make political contributions on the Partnership's behalf.
- Terminate a client without the approval of the Partner responsible for the account.
- Independently merge or sell the practice of the Partnership or sell an account.

7.3 **Vote on the Election and Termination of the Managing Partner:** A meeting for the purpose of electing or removing the Managing Partner shall be held after written notice at least ten (10) days in advance specifying the hour and purpose of the meeting.

*Executive Committee*

7.4 **Executive Committee:** There shall be an Executive Committee composed of not less than three (3) and not more than five (5) Partners as determined by the Partners at the annual meeting, plus the Managing Partner. The Executive Committee shall be chaired by the Managing Partner, and it shall appoint a Secretary for each fiscal year of the Partnership. All Executive Committee meetings shall be open to all Partners.

The Managing Partner shall preside over meetings of the Executive Committee and the Partnership, prepare an agenda for all meetings, and perform such other duties consistent with the office of Chairman as the Executive Committee shall prescribe. The Secretary shall keep the Partnership advised of actions of the Executive Committee through the keeping of minutes of Executive Committee meetings and shall perform such other duties as the Managing Partner or Executive Committee shall prescribe. The Secretary shall provide each Partner with a copy of all such minutes promptly after the meeting.

The duties and authority of the Executive Committee are as follows:

- Establishing firm policies, procedures, and long-range plans
- Developing firm goals, budgets, and objectives
- Recommending amendments to this Agreement
- Meeting on a regular basis with the Managing Partner to review firm operations and activities to assure compliance with firm policies and to monitor the firm's progress
- Recommending mergers with other accounting firms, acquisitions of accounting firms, admission of new Partners and the removal, with or without cause, of a Partner from the Partnership
- Maintaining proper staffing levels by hiring professional staff; determining salary levels, salary increases, and benefit packages; and providing staff assignments and advancements
- Determining the firm's capital requirements
- Appointing such committees as it may deem necessary to conduct the activities of the Partnership
- Delegating authority to others from time to time and recalling at any time the authority so delegated

7.5     **Election and Term:**   Members of the Executive Committee shall be elected by a majority vote of all votes cast for a two- (2-) year term at the annual Partner meeting. The Partners may serve on the Executive Committee for more than one (1) term.

7.6     **Interim Vacancies:**   When a vacancy occurs on the Executive Committee between annual meetings of the Partners, the Partnership shall, within thirty (30) days after such vacancy occurs, conduct a special meeting and elect a Partner to fill the vacancy, with said Partner to serve until the next annual meeting.

*FOR DISCUSSION PURPOSES ONLY*

7.7    **Meetings:**  The Executive Committee shall hold regular monthly meetings on the fourth (4th) Wednesday of each month. In addition, special meetings shall be called by any member of the Executive Committee as needed.

7.8    **Quorum:**  The presence of all members of the Executive Committee shall be required to constitute a quorum.

7.9    **Voting:**  Each member of the Executive Committee shall have one vote on all matters brought before the Executive Committee. If all members of the Executive Committee cannot agree on an issue, said issue may be referred to the Partnership by the dissenting member(s) for a vote at its next meeting.

7.10   **Removal:**  Members of the Executive Committee may be removed from office upon either the recommendation of a majority of the Executive Committee or the written petition of twenty-five percent (25%) of the Partners, provided that such recommendation or petition is adopted by a majority of the Partners.

# ARTICLE VIII
## MEETINGS AND VOTING

8.1    **Meetings:**  The Partners' annual meeting shall be held at a time and place to be specified by the Managing Partner in writing at least _____ (____) days before the scheduled meeting.

Regular Partnership meetings shall be held on the last Friday of each calendar month at such time as may be agreed upon by a majority of the Partners. In addition, a meeting of Partners shall be held at any time on call of the Managing Partner or at any time after written notice at least _____ (____) days in advance jointly signed by any two Partners, specifying the date, time, and purpose of the meeting. The call by the Managing Partner may be written or oral and need not be made any period of time in advance of the meeting, nor need it specify the purposes of the meeting.

*FOR DISCUSSION PURPOSES ONLY*

Minutes of each Partnership meeting shall be distributed to the Partners within _____ (____) days after the meeting.

8.2   **General Voting:**   Each Partner shall have an equal voice in the management of the Partnership, with each Partner having one (1) vote, which can be cast either in person or by proxy. Unless otherwise specified herein and assuming a quorum is present, all decisions shall be made by a majority vote of the Partners, provided no such determination shall be contrary to a provision of law or of this Agreement.

8.3   **Decisions Requiring Higher Vote:**   Except as otherwise provided herein, the following decisions shall not be made without a two-thirds (⅔) vote of the Partners, cast either in person or by proxy, assuming a quorum is present.

- Use of Partnership credit or capital in any other business
- Incurrence by the Partnership of any obligation or debt exceeding _____ dollars ($____) (exclusive of interest)
- Election or removal of Managing Partner
- Admission or expulsion of a Partner
- The sale of assets in excess of _____ dollars ($____)
- Merger with another accounting firm or firms
- Relocation of the Partnership's principal office or the opening of any Partnership office
- Compromise of any amount due to the Partnership of more than _____ dollars ($____)
- Repeal or modification of any provisions of this Agreement

8.4   **Vote by Proxy:**   Partners may vote by proxy; however, any proxy must be in writing and must specifically identify the meeting or matter to which the proxy applies. Any proxy shall be revocable at any time and shall be ineffective at any meeting at which the Partner giving such proxy is in attendance.

8.5   **Quorum:**   A majority of the Partners, either in person or by proxy, shall constitute a quorum. Each Partner shall have one (1) vote and, except as otherwise provided herein, a majority of votes cast shall determine any issue.

*FOR DISCUSSION PURPOSES ONLY*

8.6   **Unanimous Consent:**   A Partner may recommend, in place of a meeting, that the Partnership authorize an action pursuant to any provision of this Agreement by unanimous written consent of all Partners. A Partner may indicate his written consent by signing a counterpart of the proposal or by submitting a separate writing, e.g., telegram, telex, or telecopy, that specifically identifies the proposal and states that he consents to such proposal.

8.7   **Disqualification From Voting:**   Partners shall be barred from voting on any matter that affects their status as members of the Partnership, and their vote shall have no influence when determining whether a quorum is present for the purpose of acting on such matter or calculating the percentage of votes required to approve or defeat such matter.

8.8   **Right to Vote:**   Except as provided in Sections 8.2 and 8.7, no Partner shall be disqualified from voting on any issue, notwithstanding any interest he may have therein which differs from the interest of the firm or the other Partners.

8.9   **Emergency Meetings:**   If Partners who could authorize Partnership action at a duly called meeting reasonably determine, in writing, that an emergency situation is confronting the Partnership, such Partners may, without adhering to customary procedures for meetings or actions by unanimous consent, authorize any action that they consider reasonably necessary to enable the Partnership to take advantage of an opportunity or to protect the Partnership from damage, provided that they make reasonable efforts to confer with all Partners concerning such action and the reasons why such action must be taken without adhering to customary procedures.

# ARTICLE IX

## DUTIES AND RESPONSIBILITIES

9.1   **Duties of Partners:**   Each Partner shall expend on Partnership matters, a minimum of _____ (___) hours per week, based upon a yearly average, inclusive of vacations,

*FOR DISCUSSION PURPOSES ONLY*

holidays, and illness. This provision shall not be deemed to prohibit the following, so long as the activity does not substantially interfere with Partner's professional responsibilities or Partner's business and does not conflict with this Agreement:

- Writing articles, books, and other publications or delivering speeches or other addresses. However, if such activities are related to Partnership activities, any compensation received for such services shall be paid to the Partnership.

- Contributing, on the Partnership's behalf, to charitable, religious, political, and educational organizations sums up to _____ dollars ($____). Donations of greater value shall require approval by the Managing Partner.

- With the Managing Partner's approval, serving as a trustee, director, executor, or other fiduciary. Unless the Partner provides such services on behalf of the estate of a close relative, any compensation received shall be paid to the Partnership.

- With the Managing Partner's approval, holding public or civic office, or position or office with professional or charitable organizations. Any compensation received for such services shall be paid to the Partnership. This provision also applies to a Partner's spouse and minor children.

9.2 **Partner's Authority to Act on Partnership's Behalf:** Except as otherwise provided herein, each Partner is authorized to take the following actions to the extent that they are necessary to permit such Partner to carry on the practice of accounting:

- Accept clients on the Partnership's behalf and assume responsibility for specific matters for any Partnership client. However, it is the duty of such Partner to verify that such action will create no conflict of interest with any other client and that the engagement is consistent with the clients and affairs customarily assumed by the Partnership. In addition, such Partner must obtain the assent of any other Partner(s) who may reasonably be expected to serve such client.

- Render statements to clients for services rendered, provided that they apply to clients for whom he is responsible and that they are consistent with Section 8.3.

- Provide opinions as to any accounting matter, provided that at least _____ (____) other Partner(s) review(s) and concur(s) with any nonroutine opinion.
- Approve, on the Partnership's behalf, routine advances and incidental expenses, consistent with Section 8.3, necessary to the representation of a client in those matters where the Partnership has accepted responsibility.

9.3 **Conflict of Interest:** The Partners shall not engage, either directly or indirectly, as an owner, employee, consultant, or otherwise in any activity that competes with the Partnership's business and activities unless authorized by a unanimous vote of the Partners.

9.4 **Investments:** Each Partner agrees to disclose and make available to the Partnership each and every business opportunity that such Partner becomes aware of in his capacity as a Partner. However, no such disclosure or offer shall be required with respect to business opportunities that are not within the scope of the Partnership.

Each Partner shall be accountable to, and hold in trust for, the Partnership any income, compensation, or profit that such Partner may derive from any such activity, and such Partner will indemnify the Partnership for any profits that the Partnership may reasonably be viewed as having foregone or any loss that it may incur as a result of any failure by such Partner to disclose business opportunities to the Partnership.

9.5 **Restrictions on Partners' Actions:** No Partner shall act on behalf of the Partnership; mortgage, lease, or encumber Partnership property; or confess any judgment on behalf of the Partnership, without the express written authority of the Managing Partner.

9.6 **Transactions With Employees:** No Partner shall participate, or cause the Partnership to participate, in any transaction(s) with Partnership employees, other than those which will arise in the usual course of Partnership business.

*FOR DISCUSSION PURPOSES ONLY*

9.7     **Transfer Restrictions:**   No Partner shall sell, mortgage, assign, transfer, or in any other manner dispose of, alienate, or encumber any or all of his Partnership interest or any rights therein without the prior written, unanimous consent of the Partners. Any transfer not in conformity with this provision shall be null and void and shall confer no rights on the transferee as against the Partnership or as against the other Partners. Recognizing the purposes of the Partnership and the relationship among the Partners, each Partner acknowledges that such transfer restrictions are reasonable and shall be specifically enforceable. Each Partner further agrees to hold both the Partnership and each Partner (and each Partner's successors and assigns) completely harmless from any damage, liability, or cost, sustained by any such indemnified persons as a result of a transfer or an attempted transfer in violation of this Agreement.

9.8     **Enforcement of Transfers:**   In the event that the other Partners shall consent to the transfer and subject to the transfer restrictions contained herein, such transfer shall be made expressly subject to all terms and conditions of this Agreement and shall be binding on the respective successors, assigns, and personal representatives of the Partners.

9.9     **Indemnification:**   Each Partner shall indemnify and hold harmless the Partnership and each Partner from claims, damages, and expenses arising from his own negligence to the extent that the acts are not covered by, or the amount of damages exceeds, the Partnership's insurance coverage.

9.10    **Fees for Professional Services:**   Each Partner shall charge reasonably for all professional services rendered by him, following generally the policies of the firm as to fees charged. However, each Partner may serve professionally without charge any member of his own family or any relative and, with the consent of the Managing Partner, any Partner may serve without charge, or at less than regular charge, any educational, civic, charitable, or religious organization.

*FOR DISCUSSION PURPOSES ONLY*

No salaries, commissions, fees, or gratuities exceeding _____ dollars ($____) shall be accepted, directly or indirectly, by any Partner personally from any client or prospective client of the firm, without the express consent in advance of the Managing Partner, and the fair value of any such item received with such consent, though retained by the Partner, shall be treated for accounting purposes as compensation to the firm and shall be charged against such Partner as an advance on the next maturing installment or installments of his drawing account. The Managing Partner may agree, however, to any exception to any provision of this Section.

9.11 **Professional Obligations:** At the expense of the Partnership, each Partner shall—

- Maintain memberships in good standing in the American Institute of Certified Public Accountants and the [state] Society of Certified Public Accountants.
- Maintain full effectiveness of his license to practice in [state].

Each Partner will at all times comply with all of the provisions of the Code of Professional Conduct as adopted by the American Institute of Certified Public Accountants and by the statutes, rules, and regulations of the state society and the board of public accountancy covering all professional services that he shall render.

9.12 **Memberships in Professional or Civic Organizations:** Partners are encouraged to belong to Partnership-approved professional organizations. As a customary expense of its business that is deductible before determination of net profits, the Partnership shall pay dues and provide Partners with membership in those professional or civic organizations that enhance the practice of accountancy.

9.13 **Automobile:** Each Partner shall furnish and maintain a suitable automobile to the extent necessary to properly discharge his duties to the Partnership and shall carry on such travel, continuing professional education, and client-firm relations activities, including entertainment and membership in social,

*FOR DISCUSSION PURPOSES ONLY*

civic, and business clubs, as are consistent with the development of his portion of the professional practice of the firm.

Each Partner shall be responsible for the maintenance of suitable insurance coverage on his own automobile or automobiles, which insurance shall provide automobile liability coverage of not less than _____ dollars ($____) per person and _____ dollars ($____) per accident for bodily injury and/or death and _____ dollars ($____) for property damage, or a combined single limit or _____ dollars ($____), or such other coverage as may from time to time be required to meet the underlying primary liability insurance requirements of the umbrella policy of insurance provided by the Partnership.

9.14   **Expenses:**   Expenses incurred by Partners in furtherance of Partnership business are subject to reimbursement. However, the firm will not reimburse Partners for those expenses that Partners are required to incur on the firm's behalf, such as home entertainment for clients, home telephone expenses, and gift contributions.

9.15   **Wills:**   In his will, each Partner shall instruct his executor to adhere to the terms of this Agreement and sell his Partnership interest. However, a Partner's failure to direct his executor in this regard shall not affect the legality or enforceability of this Agreement.

# ARTICLE X

## FINANCIAL MANAGEMENT

10.1   **Books of Account:**   The Partnership shall maintain, at its principal office, comprehensive books of account for the Partnership which shall show an accurate record of all transactions of the Partnership and its condition as well as the names and addresses of the Partners. The Partnership shall keep its records and file all Partnership income tax returns using the cash method of accounting but shall periodically prepare financial statements and make all financial determinations under this Agreement in accordance with generally accepted accounting principles. Each Partner, or his legal representative, shall, at his sole expense, have the right, upon reasonable notice and at reasonable times, to examine, copy, and audit the Partnership's books and records.

10.2 **Method of Accounting:** The Partnership's books of account shall be kept on a cash basis.

10.3 **Fiscal Year:** The Partnership's fiscal year shall be the year ending _____.

10.4 **Tax Returns:** The Partnership tax returns shall be filed on a cash basis, and each Partner shall be furnished, within _____ (____) days after the close of each fiscal year of the Partnership, with a copy of each tax return and any other information which each Partner may require in connection with each Partner's own tax matters.

Each Partner shall timely file his own personal tax return and submit copies to the Partnership.

10.5 **Operating Statements:** An operating statement shall be prepared and submitted to each Partner at the close of each calendar month. The statement shall set forth Partnership operations for the preceding month.

10.6 **Partner Reports:** The Partnership shall provide each Partner, within _____ (____) days after the close of each fiscal year, with a copy of the Partnership's financial statements. The Partnership's accountants shall review such statements.

Unless written objection is made by a Partner within _____ (____) days after actual receipt of such financial statements, each such annual accounting shall constitute an accord and satisfaction, and a release and discharge as of the end of such year of all claims not reflected in such statements which any Partner has against the Partnership or against any other Partner arising out of the operation of the Partnership.

*FOR DISCUSSION PURPOSES ONLY*

**10.7  Adoption of Financial Statements and Tax Returns:**   Each Partner shall have _____ (____) days after receipt to dispute the Partnership tax return and financial statement, after which time such tax return and financial statement will be deemed binding.

**10.8  Banking:**   All Partnership funds shall be deposited in its name, in such checking accounts or similar accounts with member banks of the FDIC as approved by the Partners. Partnership funds shall not be commingled with the funds of any other person or entity.

**10.9  Tax Matters Partner:**   The Partnership designates _____ as the party to receive notices from the Internal Revenue Service which pertain to the Partnership's tax affairs, and he shall be the "Tax Matters Partner" pursuant to the Code. The Tax Matters Partner shall be reimbursed for all reasonable expenses incurred as a result of his duties as Tax Matters Partner. If _____ should resign as Tax Matters Partner or as a general Partner, or his entire Partnership interest is disposed of or terminated, _____ shall become the Tax Matters Partner.

# ARTICLE XI

## RESTRICTIONS TO PRACTICE

**11.1  Noncompetition—Retirees:**   A Partner who retires from the Partnership shall not, during such period as he may be receiving any payments as a retired Partner, solicit or perform, either individually or as a member of a partnership or as an employee of an individual, partnership, or corporation, professional services, such as auditing, accounting, management services, tax, or any other services customarily rendered by the Partnership. Any retired Partner who breaches this provision shall no longer be entitled to receive further retirement payments.

**11.2  Noncompetition—Resigning Partners:**   A Partner who withdraws from the Partnership shall not, for a period of _____ (____) years after withdrawal, solicit or perform,

*FOR DISCUSSION PURPOSES ONLY*

either individually or as a member of a partnership or as an employee of an individual, partnership, or corporation, professional services, such as auditing, accounting, management services, tax, or any other services customarily rendered by the Partnership, within a _____ (____) mile radius of the city or cities where an office of the Partnership is located at the time of the Partner's resignation or within _____ (____) years prior thereto. In the case of a national Partner, he shall be deemed to have conducted a major part of his activities in both the city in which his regular office was located and in the city in which the principal office was located during his period of service as a national Partner.

Should a court of competent jurisdiction determine that the enforcement of this provision is unreasonable in terms of time or geographic area and that a more limited provision would be reasonable, it is intended that the more limited provision determined by the court to be reasonable shall be given effect.

Should a withdrawn Partner provide such service, he shall pay the Partnership an amount equal to the average annual fee earned by the Partnership for the _____ (____) year period preceding the date of his withdrawal. If the Partnership had served the client for less than _____ (____) years preceding the date of such withdrawal, the payment to the Partnership shall be an amount equal to the average annual accrual fee determined on the basis of the shorter period.

Partnership clients are defined for purposes of this article to include those persons or entities for whom professional services were rendered by the Partnership within _____ (____) months preceding the date of such withdrawal.

# ARTICLE XII

## DISPUTE RESOLUTION, DISSOLUTION, AND WINDING UP

12.1 **Mediation:**   Any controversy or claim which arises under the terms of this Agreement and which is not resolved through negotiation shall be settled by mediation in accordance with the current Commercial Mediation Rules of the American Arbitration Association before resorting to arbitration, litigation, or some other dispute resolution procedure. The costs of mediation shall be shared equally by the parties to the dispute.

12.2 **Arbitration:**   Any controversy or claim which arises under the terms of this Agreement and which is not resolved through negotiation or mediation shall be settled by arbitration in accordance with the current Commercial Arbitration Rules of the American Arbitration Association, and judgment upon the award rendered by the arbitrator(s) may be entered in any court having jurisdiction thereof. The costs of arbitration shall be allocated among the parties as directed by the arbitrators.

12.3 **Attorney's Fees:**   If any legal action is instituted to enforce the provisions of this Agreement, the prevailing party shall be entitled to receive, in addition to such other relief as may be granted, reasonable attorney's fees and costs.

12.4 **Dissolution:**   The Partnership shall dissolve and be terminated on or upon the earlier happening of any one of the following:

- The unanimous written consent of the Partners
- The occurrence of any event which, under the Act or as otherwise provided by law, causes a dissolution or termination of the Partnership
- Any event which results in there being only one (1) Partner

Promptly upon dissolution, a Notice of Dissolution shall be published under the [*governing state*] Corporation Code or any equivalent successor statute.

The Partners shall share in profits and losses during the liquidation period in the same proportions in which they shared profits and losses prior to the termination of the Partnership business.

*FOR DISCUSSION PURPOSES ONLY*

12.5 **Winding Up:**  Upon the dissolution of the Partnership, the Partners shall designate a Liquidator of the Partnership who shall, with reasonable speed, wind up Partnership business, sell all Partnership property, and distribute the proceeds of liquidation in the following manner:

- First, pay all debts to creditors other than Partners.
- Second, pay all debts to Partners, other than capital loans to Partners.
- Third, pay all capital loans to Partners.
- Fourth, distribute to Partners the balances of their capital accounts. If any Partner's capital account has a deficit balance, such Partner shall contribute to the capital of the Partnership.
- Fifth, allocate any remaining funds among present Partners in proportion to their capital accounts prior to dissolution.

Partners shall act in a fashion that is consistent with the winding up of the Partnership's business and affairs. The Liquidator shall comply with all requirements of the Act and other applicable laws pertaining to the winding up of a partnership, following which the Partnership shall stand liquidated and terminated. Partners shall receive no additional compensation for any services performed pursuant to this provision.

12.6 **Rights of Partners:**  Except as otherwise provided herein, Partners are restricted to the Partnership's assets for the return of their capital contributions, and they shall have no right to receive value other than cash from the Partnership.

12.7 **Files and Workpapers:**  Each Partner agrees that files shall be maintained for the purpose of retaining copies of income tax returns, financial statements, and other documents prepared and issued by the Partnership, together with the attendant worksheets. The Partnership, not the individual Partners, shall have title to and ownership of such files.

In connection with the winding up and liquidation of the Partnership, the Partner who regularly rendered professional services to the client shall be entitled to the client's files, unless the client requests otherwise.

A Partner who withdraws from the Partnership and intends to or does continue to practice public accounting shall be entitled only to the files of those clients for whom he regularly performed professional services while a member of the Partnership and for whom he will regularly perform professional services after his withdrawal from the Partnership.

The deceased Partner's estate shall not be entitled to any Partnership records, other than those relating to personal matters of the deceased Partner.

12.8 **Confidential Relationship:** It shall be the duty of the Partners and of any arbitrators appointed pursuant to this Agreement to maintain in confidence, to the greatest extent reasonably possible, any and all information relating to the professional affairs of the Partnership and any and all information as to any differences of opinion which may from time to time arise between the Partners relating to the professional affairs of the Partnership or to the management or conduct thereof.

# ARTICLE XIII

## MISCELLANEOUS

13.1 **Binding Effect:** This Agreement shall be binding upon and inure to the benefit of the respective Partners and all future Partners of this firm who are admitted to the Partnership in accordance with its terms and provisions. Each Partner binds and obligates himself, his spouse or estate, and any and all persons claiming by, through, or under him. No person shall have any rights or obligations relating to the Partnership greater than those set forth in this Agreement, and no person shall acquire an interest in the Partnership or become a Partner except as permitted by the terms of this Agreement.

*FOR DISCUSSION PURPOSES ONLY*

13.2 **Amendments:** This Agreement may be amended, modified, or revoked in whole or in part by a two-thirds (⅔) vote of the Partners. No amendment, modification, or revocation shall become effective until it has been reduced to writing and signed by all Partners.

13.3 **Governing Law:** This Agreement shall be governed by and construed in accordance with the laws of the state of _____ .

13.4 **Notices:** Any notice, payment, demand, offer and acceptance, or other communication (collectively referred to as "notice") required or permitted pursuant to this Agreement shall be in writing and shall be deemed to have been duly given on the date of service if served personally upon the Partner to whom notice is given; or on the second business day after mailing if mailed to the Partner to whom notice is to be given, by first class mail, postage prepaid, and addressed to the addressee at the address designated herein; or on the first business day after it is transmitted if telegraphed, telexed, or express mailed to the addressee at the address designated herein. Any Partner may change his address by giving written notice to the Partnership, to the attention of the Managing Partner. Notices to the Partnership shall similarly be given and addressed to it at its principal place of business.

13.5 **Construction:** Every provision, term, and covenant of this Agreement shall be construed according to its fair meaning and not strictly for or against any Partner.

13.6 **Usage:** Wherever from the context it appears appropriate, references to the masculine shall include the feminine and neuter; the feminine shall include the masculine and neuter; the neuter shall include the masculine and feminine; the singular shall include the plural; and the plural shall include the singular.

13.7 **Headings:** The captions included in this Agreement are for reference purposes only and shall not affect the interpretation of this Agreement.

*FOR DISCUSSION PURPOSES ONLY*

13.8  **Severability:**  Every provision of this Agreement is intended to be severable. If any provision, term, covenant, or condition of this Agreement or application thereof to any person or circumstance is held invalid, the remainder of the Agreement shall remain in full force and effect, and shall be interpreted as though such provision were not included herein.

13.9  **Entire Agreement:**  This Agreement contains the entire agreement of the Partners with respect to its subject matter and supersedes any and all prior negotiations, understandings, and agreements with regard hereto. Any oral representations or modifications shall be unenforceable unless reduced to writing and signed by the Partner to be charged.

13.10  **Incorporation by Reference:**  Every exhibit and schedule attached to this Agreement and referred to herein is incorporated into this Agreement by reference.

13.11  **Counterparts:**  This Agreement may be executed in multiple counterparts, each of which shall be an original, but all of which, when taken together, shall be deemed one and the same instrument.

Should it become necessary to introduce into evidence before any court or other tribunal the text of this Agreement, it shall not be necessary to offer evidence of the execution of this Agreement by any party other than the party against whom, or by whom, it is sought to enforce the provisions of this Agreement.

13.12  **Waiver:**  Failure or delay of either party in exercising any right or remedy under this Agreement, or any other agreement between them, or otherwise, will not operate as a waiver thereof. The express waiver by any party of a breach of any provision of this Agreement by the other party shall not operate or be construed as a waiver of any subsequent breach of said party. No waiver shall be effective until it is reduced to writing and signed by the waiving party.

13.13  **Further Acts:**  Each Partner shall perform all further acts and execute, acknowledge, and deliver any documents which may be reasonably necessary, appropriate, or desirable to carry out the provisions of this Agreement.

*FOR DISCUSSION PURPOSES ONLY*

**13.14 Third-Party Claims:** This Agreement shall solely benefit the parties to this Agreement and their affiliates. No other person shall be able to enforce or make any claims pursuant to its provisions.

**13.15 Indemnification:** If a final judgment is levied against the Partnership, which becomes a lien against the property of a Partner(s), or if any Partner(s) is required to pay such judgment, the Partnership shall secure the discharge of such lien and shall indemnify such Partner(s) with respect to such payment.

**13.16 Equitable Remedies:** In addition to other available rights, each Partner shall have the right of specific performance, injunction, and other equitable remedy in the event of any actual or threatened breach of this Agreement, the parties acknowledging that the Partnership has no adequate remedy at law.

**13.17 Incorporation of Partner:** Any Partner may incorporate pursuant to the rules and regulations promulgated by the [*governing state*] Board of Accountancy. The newly created professional accounting corporation shall then be admitted as a Partner to the Partnership in lieu of the individual Partner.

IN WITNESS WHEREOF, the parties have caused this Agreement of Partnership to be executed as of the date first set forth above.

_____
Joseph F. Delong

_____
Anton E. Wagner

_____
Martha A. Bonner

_____
Dorothy M. Convery

_____
R. Blane Holmes

*FOR DISCUSSION PURPOSES ONLY*

The undersigned, as spouses of Joseph F. Delong, Anton E. Wagner, Martha A. Bonner, Dorothy M. Convery, and R. Blane Holmes, hereby sign the above Partnership Agreement for the purpose of binding themselves thereto.

_____

Elizabeth A. Delong

_____

Mary F. Wagner

_____

George J. Bonner

_____

William F. Convery

_____

Sherry W. Holmes

# III
# PROFESSIONAL CORPORATIONS

## BACKGROUND

Professional corporations are formal legal entities that are created by following governing statutes. They can enter contracts, acquire assets, hire employees, and be held liable for their debts.

The two most common methods of incorporating your practice are to have the owners transfer cash and assets to the corporation in return for stock or, if your accounting practice has been conducted as a partnership, to have the partnership transfer its assets and liabilities to the corporation in return for stock, which will then be distributed to the former partners in proportion to their partnership interests.

Conducting your accounting practice as a professional corporation neither begins nor ends with transferring assets in return for stock or meeting initial statutory requirements. It begins with your first attempt at planning and preparing for your corporate organization and continues throughout your corporate existence

53

by observing corporate procedures and formalities. A professional corporation's failure to maintain its corporate "form" may result in challenges by the IRS and other third parties.

# CORPORATE DOCUMENTS

## Introduction

Creating and maintaining your professional accounting corporation requires adherence to a variety of organizational documents, specifically, articles of incorporation, bylaws, employment contracts, and buy-sell agreements. This section discusses the content and effect of these documents and allows you to work more closely and effectively with your attorney, resulting in incorporation documents that are legally enforceable and reflective of your professional goals and personal practice philosophy. However, this discussion does not necessarily identify all documents that may be needed for the incorporation of your practice. An attorney experienced in both corporation and income tax laws should be retained to confirm your choice of agreements and verify their content. Documents must adhere to and be consistent with the requirements of your state's professional and business corporation acts and the rules of regulatory agencies. Compliance with these statutory and professional mandates can best be achieved with the assistance of counsel. A discussion of the legal and ethical requirements involved in the organization of your accounting practice is included in chapter IV, "The Lawyer's Role in Your Accounting Partnership or Professional Corporation."

## Articles of Incorporation

Serving as a contract between the corporation and its shareholders, between the state and the corporation, and among the shareholders, the articles of incorporation set forth the corporation's professional boundaries. Frequently referred to as the charter, the articles function as the corporation's constitution by defining the rights and duties of shareholders and directors and by charting the corporation's professional direction. When deciding where to include any provisions of a limiting or specific nature that can be placed in either your articles of incorporation or bylaws, you should remember that provisions included in the articles are difficult to change; therefore, greater flexibility would be achieved by placing these particular provisions in your bylaws. Bylaws can usually be changed by an action of the board of directors. The article's prominent position in the corporate scheme is illustrated by the fact that when drafting questions or conflicts arise, the articles of incorporation prevail over inconsistent provisions contained in the bylaws or private agreements.

The practitioner's role in the incorporation process does not end when the articles of incorporation are drafted. Once reduced to writing, the articles must be signed and acknowledged in a manner consistent with your state's business corporation act. Every state requires that the articles of incorporation be filed with a filing fee and recorded with the state official who administers the state's corporation laws, usually the secretary of state. It may be that your articles can be executed on an official form provided by the appropriate state official. This filing requirement not only makes your articles of incorporation the most public of your corporate documents, but, pending approval, it also signifies the beginning of your corporate existence. Finally, some states require you to publish your notice of incorporation, usually once but sometimes more frequently, in a newspaper of general circulation, a legal newspaper, or both.

The major issues that should be addressed by your articles of incorporation include—

- Corporate name.
- Corporate purpose (most jurisdictions allow a corporation to pursue any legal purpose).
- Profession to be practiced.
- Address of registered office.
- Names and addresses of directors and incorporators.
- Requirement that each shareholder be licensed to practice.
- Duration of corporate existence.

- Number of shares of stock the corporation has authority to issue.
- Voting rights of the stock.
- Restrictions on the alienability of shares to nonprofessionals.
- Name and address of the corporation's registered agent.

Please refer to appendix A for sample articles of incorporation.

## Bylaws

Accountants are required to draft bylaws when incorporating their practices. Serving as a supplement to the articles of incorporation and as general organizational rules, bylaws govern the affairs of the corporation and are binding upon the members of the corporation. Specifically, they delineate the rights, responsibilities, and authority of shareholders, officers, directors, employees, and agents, and they include information that is not included in the publicly filed articles of incorporation. To facilitate the drafting of bylaws that accurately reflect your corporate structure, first identify management functions and construct a comprehensive organizational chart depicting the functions of and relationships among members of your professional corporation.

The major issues that should be addressed by your bylaws include—

- Duties of corporate officers and directors.
- Methods of electing, removing, and replacing officers and directors.
- Requisite number of directors.
- Time, place, and frequency of shareholders' and directors' meetings.
- Quorum requirements and the rules governing meetings.
- Voting.
- Procedures for amending bylaws.
- Fiscal year and accounting method.

Please refer to appendix B for sample bylaws.

## Employment Contracts

A key document for any accountant planning to incorporate a practice is the employment contract. It solidifies the professional relationship between the corporation and its shareholder-employees. The salient points of the contract should be identified and the document completed prior to the filing of the articles of incorporation. Due to the diverse positions held by the professionals on your staff, the employment contract can be written to meet individual needs, such as those of a senior officer who is approaching retirement, or of a newly elected officer or a staff accountant who is not yet a shareholder. In all cases, it should be completed before employment begins.

The positive result of including employment contracts in your incorporation process is not limited to fulfilling the legal obligations between the practitioner and the corporation; in addition, it promotes your firm's corporate appearance and makes a clear and definitive statement about what the employee and the corporation can expect to receive from one another. Fostering a sense of organization and stability among your staff, employment contracts provide motivation, encouragement, and peace of mind to all professionals in the firm.

The major issues that should be addressed by your employment contracts include—

- Term of employment.
- Compensation and bonuses.
- Fringe benefits.
- Employees' responsibilities and activities.
- Vacation allotments.
- Leaves of absence.
- Definition of full-time employment and provision for part-time employment.
- Time devoted to corporation.
- Corporate control clause.
- Covenant not to compete (as authorized by statute).
- Corporate opportunity.
- Life, liability, and malpractice insurance.

- Expense reimbursement for education, professional dues, insurance, travel, entertainment, and home office.
- Access to corporate records.
- Prohibition against assignment of the contract.
- Acts causing termination.
- Conditions for total, partial, temporary, and permanent disability.
- Compensation and benefits upon disability, death, retirement, or termination.
- Early/late retirement.
- Assumption of liabilities in the event of corporate sale, liquidation, or merger.
- Arbitration as a dispute resolution procedure.

Please refer to appendix C for a sample employment contract.

Retirement benefits either constitute a prominent portion of your employment contract or serve as a separate retirement or deferred-income contract. Outgoing shareholders may have included in their payments the value of goodwill as well as accounts receivable and work-in-process if they have not been provided for in the value of the shares of stock. Benefit formulas frequently vary, although it is not difficult to calculate the benefit. This results in proper compensation to an employee for value not included in the retirement of corporate stock.

The major issues that should be addressed by your retirement or deferred-income contract include—

- Date when payments begin.
- Amount, frequency, and duration of payments.
- Number of guaranteed years that payments will be made.
- Provision for naming a beneficiary in writing prior to employee's death.
- Adjustments to payments consistent with cost-of-living index.

## Buy-Sell Agreements

Accountants incorporating their practices find it necessary to draft buy-sell agreements that provide a definitive policy for the disposition of withdrawing or deceased shareholders' stock. These agreements are typically activated upon a shareholder's retirement, incapacity, death prior to retirement, and voluntary or involuntary withdrawal from employment. Buy-sell agreements can take two forms:

1. Stock redemption agreement, which provides that upon the withdrawal or death of a shareholder, the shareholder or his estate will offer to sell his stock directly to the corporation. Though it is usually recommended, the corporation is not obligated to purchase the shares.

2. Cross-purchase agreement, which provides that upon the withdrawal or death of a shareholder, the shareholder or his estate will offer to sell his stock directly to the remaining shareholders. As is usually the case with stock redemption agreements, shareholders are not obligated to purchase the shares.

A professional accounting corporation can achieve heightened flexibility through a combined stock-redemption and cross-purchase agreement whereby the withdrawing or deceased shareholder's first responsibility is to offer the shares to the corporation and then to offer any unpurchased shares to the remaining shareholders. This degree of flexibility can also be achieved by first offering the shares to the remaining shareholders and then offering the unpurchased shares to the corporation. If the objective of a buy-sell agreement is to trigger a sale, the corporation or the remaining shareholders must be obligated to purchase the remaining shares; otherwise, corporate sale or liquidation would likely result.

Practitioners functioning without a buy-sell agreement in force proceed at their own peril, much as does an individual who forsakes the advice of others to prepare a will. Legislation has been enacted throughout the country, and its purpose is consistent with the intent of buy-sell agreements; however, the methods used to achieve this purpose are imposed by statute and are not determined by the shareholders to whom they apply. Some states require that the corporation's articles of incorporation or bylaws contain a provision addressing stock disposition upon the withdrawal or death of a shareholder, while others place restrictions on the transfer of shares or mandate the transfer to qualified persons within a specific time period. Prevailing in some jurisdictions is a specific statutory guideline that determines the distribution of shares when the issue is not addressed by the articles of incorporation, bylaws, or other private agreements. This discussion clearly indicates that if the accountant fails to assume responsibility for stock disposition, state law will control, resulting in the disposition of shares to the satisfaction of the state legislature, though not necessarily to that of the shareholder or the shareholder's estate.

Including a well-designed buy-sell agreement in the organization of your professional accounting corporation is a recommended approach to practice management since it—

- Provides a deceased stockholder's estate with the liquidity necessary to meet taxes and related expenses.
- Places a value on withdrawing or deceased stockholders' shares of stock, resulting, in the case of a deceased stockholder, in an established value for estate tax purposes.
- Maintains corporate cohesion by preventing a shareholder from transferring stock to an unacceptable party.
- Heightens shareholder awareness of the funding necessary for the eventual purchase of shares of withdrawing and deceased shareholders.
- Satisfies the conflicting demands of the deceased stockholder's estate or withdrawing stockholder and the remaining stockholders.
- Provides a way to terminate a practice relationship.

It is therefore vital that all aspects of your buy-sell agreement be carefully considered by the shareholders, since it is only by means of a complete, accurate agreement that the corporate shareholders can control the terms of redemption.

The major issues that should be addressed by your buy-sell agreement include—

- Price, and method of computing the price, at which the shares of a deceased or withdrawing shareholder will be purchased and sold.
- Restrictions on stock transfers.
- Corporation's right-of-first-refusal of stock that a shareholder desires to sell or assign.
- Termination of voting rights upon shareholder's withdrawal or death.
- Endorsement imposed on stock certificate.
- Behavior resulting in termination.
- Requirement of new shareholders to execute agreement.

Please refer to appendix D for a sample buy-sell agreement.

A final point to consider is the admission of a new shareholder. After an employee has worked for your firm for a number of years, you may wish to make the employee a stockholder. The two methods used to accomplish this are:

1. The corporation issues the employee additional shares of stock, the number of which represents the employee's percentage of ownership, or
2. The stockholders transfer to the employee the appropriate number of shares in return for the employee's payment for the stock.

## PROFESSIONAL CORPORATION PRACTICES

In addition to external changes, the incorporation of your practice will result in internal changes, specifically, changes in the operation of your firm. The individuals responsible for the outcome of those decisions vested within the corporation and not controlled by statute are the directors and officers. Elected annually by shareholders, directors generally need not possess any particular qualifications and need not even be shareholders unless they are required to be by your articles of incorporation. However, most state regulations require all shareholders to be certified public accountants licensed to practice in that jurisdiction. Management of corporate affairs rests with the board of directors, and their responsibilities generally entail overseeing the officers' daily activities and establishing their compensation, formulating corporate policy, authorizing corporate contracts, and declaring dividends. Directors are frequently compensated for their services, although this is not mandatory. In their capacity as directors, they can be sued; therefore, corporations are advised always to have officer and director liability insurance in effect. Some jurisdictions require that at least one directors' meeting be held each year; however, this decision is frequently within the directors' discretion and addressed in the bylaws.

The officers of a corporation, consisting mainly of the president, vice president, secretary, and treasurer, are elected by the directors and are responsible for the daily administration of the professional corporation. The president exercises control over the corporation's business affairs and is vested with the authority to hire and fire employees. The vice president assumes the president's duties upon the president's absence or death. The authority to execute documents and stock certificates is usually vested in both president and vice president. The duties of the secretary and treasurer, though less austere, are by no means less vital to the professional corporation. The secretary is entrusted with maintaining corporate records and ensuring that all corporate notices are provided to persons identified in the bylaws. The treasurer maintains corporate financial records and administers federal and local withholding taxes, sales taxes, and payments.

To receive the continuing benefits of corporate practice and avoid challenges by the IRS, your accounting corporation must continuously function as a corporation, which requires adherence to corporate formalities. You must learn to think of the corporation as a separate entity and make sure that your books and records are maintained in a fashion which documents this distinction. The board of directors must hold meetings to both implement major corporate policy and discuss daily affairs. These meetings should be held at least annually and as frequently as there is business for the directors to discuss; however, directors are usually at liberty to determine when, where, and how the meetings are to be conducted. Board meetings can be classified into two categories:

1. Regular meetings which are regularly scheduled and may be held without notice

2. Special meetings which are held at any time, provided that all directors are given notice

Although the board of directors is authorized to act on any matter within the scope of the corporation's authority, the board is required to meet as a board in order to act lawfully, except in those situations where statutes permit action by written consent in place of a meeting (in these cases, unanimous approval of the action is required). Items subject to board approval include benefit plans, employment contracts, leases, and insurance matters. Despite the latitude provided by courts in enforcing board meeting requirements for professional accounting corporations, it is not recommended that informal verbal agreements be substituted for formal directors' meetings, since this could result in a challenge by the IRS alleging that the organization is not being operated as a legitimate corporation. Keep in mind that an important option held by directors is their right to dissent when the director believes that a majority of the board is acting in a questionable fashion. By filing a written dissent, recording it in the minutes, or sending it by registered mail to the secretary immediately following the meeting, the director is removed from any personal liability resulting from the board's action.

Every state's business corporation law requires that shareholders meet at least once a year; however, their failure to conduct the meeting at the designated time will not cause corporate dissolution. Usually included in the bylaws, the time and place of the annual meeting may also be contained in the articles of incorporation.

The most important actions taken at the annual shareholders' meeting are the election of directors for the forthcoming year and the review and approval of the acts of directors and officers during the preceding year. In addition to holding an annual meeting, a professional corporation may have special shareholder meetings throughout the year to address daily corporate operations. All shareholders who are entitled to vote must receive notice of shareholder meetings, and in most states, it must be in writing, signed by an officer, usually the president, and delivered within the time limit required by law. This notice includes the time and place of the meeting and a statement of the issue(s) to be discussed.

A professional corporation is required to maintain a formal record of shareholder and director actions. This is accomplished by keeping detailed written minutes of stockholder and director meetings, together with copies of documents that are acted upon at such meetings, in a corporate minute book. The secretary generally maintains the minute book, a procedure that should be followed even if there is only one shareholder or one director.

# INCORPORATION PLAN

Planning the incorporation of your accounting practice usually begins several months before the date of corporate operation; however, the exact period involved will depend upon the particular needs of the firm. When you have a clear understanding of how decisions are made, the incorporation of your practice and its subsequent maintenance can proceed in an organized, effective manner. Set forth below is one possible approach to a successful incorporation that makes clear to the public your message that a new professional accounting corporation has begun.

### SAMPLE INCORPORATION SEQUENCE

1. Hold a meeting of the CPA incorporators and their attorneys. Matters addressed at this stage include—

    - Target date.
    - Corporate name.

- Officers and directors.
- Agent to accept service of process.
- Benefit plans.
- Corporate fiscal year.
- Accounting method.
- Capitalization of the corporation, i.e., amount of stock authorized and issued.
- Classes of stock.
- Identity of stockholders (with their proportional shares).
- Determination of which assets and liabilities will be transferred to the corporation.
- Whether an S corporation election will be made.

2. Contact the secretary of state concerning the availability of the corporate name and reserve the name if necessary. Corporate designation varies among states.

3. Obtain certificates of license in those states that require certificates to accompany the articles of incorporation.

4. Draft corporate documents, including articles of incorporation, bylaws, minutes of first meeting of board of directors, stock certificates, employment contracts, benefit plan agreements, buy-sell agreements, and documents of transfer of assets and liabilities.

5. File articles of incorporation (include certificate of license if required by law).

6. Order materials, including corporate seal, stock certificates, stock register, and minute book.

7. Hold organizational meeting. Present at the meeting may be the incorporators, shareholders, or directors. Though there is no limit to the number of issues that may be decided, the more prominent tasks include—

- Electing officers.
- Determining which assets and liabilities will be turned over to the corporation.
- Adopting and executing bylaws; employment contracts; stock purchase agreements; and pension, profit-sharing, and other employee benefit plans.

- Authorizing treasurer to pay organizational expenses.
- Determining officers' compensation.
- Making necessary banking and borrowing resolutions.
- Establishing annual meeting date.
- Entering the fiscal year-end in the minutes.
- Assigning leases.
- Determining income tax elections.
- Obtaining or revising necessary insurance policies, including workers' compensation, malpractice, and liability policies.

The organizational meeting is frequently followed by the first meeting of the board of directors.

8. Prepare incorporating balance sheet, chart of accounts, new ledgers and journals, checks and other printed accounting forms, organization chart, statements of policy, and position descriptions.

9. Direct the appropriate person or organization to—

- Transfer insurance.
- File new W-4 forms.
- Obtain third-party consent for assignments of contracts and leases.
- Change name listing in telephone directory, signs, building directory, stationery, business cards, and invoices.
- Advise licensing authorities, professional societies, utilities, and other suppliers to change their accounts.

10. File final federal and state payroll tax report for predecessor practices.

11. Issue shares of stock.

*The professional incorporation checklist above is presented primarily to assist CPAs who are incorporating their own practice. It does not address the various special requirements of other professions.*

# IV
# THE LAWYER'S ROLE IN YOUR ACCOUNTING PARTNERSHIP OR PROFESSIONAL CORPORATION

## BACKGROUND

Fellow practitioners can be a valuable source of information for accountants developing their organizational documents. By participating in local practice management roundtables sponsored by the state societies and local firms and by attending state and national MAP conferences, you can learn the principles involved in preparing agreements and ways of avoiding common stumbling blocks. Further guidance can be found in the AICPA *Management of an Accounting Practice Handbook* and other practice management literature.

We can assume that the principals in a CPA firm know more than the average lawyer does about the contents of their accounting partnership agreement and incorporation documents; however, the attorney's role is crucial nonetheless. Accountants have a great deal of flexibility in structuring their organizational documents especially when they are practicing as a partnership. However, there are formalities that cannot be overlooked, specifically the Uniform Partnership Act (UPA); the Model Business Corporation Act (MBCA); local, state, and federal certification and filing requirements; and state law.

## ACCOUNTING PARTNERSHIPS AND THE UPA

To the extent that it has been adopted by the relevant jurisdictions, the definitive governing body for accountants practicing as partnerships is the UPA. The UPA codifies and reforms the common law of partnership and specifies partners' rights and obligations. In those states where the UPA is not in effect, local statutes and decisions control. A number of states have made minor modifications to the UPA. An attorney experienced in partnership law will ensure that your agreement complies with both the mandates of local and state statutes and the provisions of the UPA, thereby anticipating and avoiding points of conflict with these bodies of law.

In the resolution of conflicts within the partnership, the UPA controls only when the subject is not addressed by the partnership agreement or when the partners are unable to agree. The statute also affords protection to other individuals or entities who are strangers to the partnership, which can frequently supersede provisions of the partnership agreement. If a particular issue is not resolved to the satisfaction of a particular partner, it may be necessary to litigate the issue; however, too frequently the court's interpretation of the agreement is inconsistent with what the partners originally intended. Final external sources of governance of your partnership are case law, reports of state administrative agencies, as well as local, state, and federal certification and filing requirements.

# PROFESSIONAL CORPORATIONS: REGULATED ENTITIES

As is the case with other business ventures, the incorporation of your accounting practice requires that a wide range of decisions be made, some of which will be controlled by statute. This control has been exercised at the state level since the turn of the century, and inasmuch as these early statutes codified the state corporation law, they were plagued by inconsistencies among states. This situation was alleviated to some degree as states gradually began to enact similar corporation laws, largely as a result of the Model Business Corporation Act (MBCA), which was developed by the American Bar Association in 1950 and completely revised in 1969. However, substantive differences in corporation laws continue to exist among states with many of the important corporate jurisdictions, such as Delaware, New York, New Jersey, California, and Michigan, choosing not to base their corporation laws on the MBCA. The MBCA remains under consideration in some other states. In addition to the ABA's influence, the Securities Act of 1933 and the Securities Exchange Act of 1934 have affected corporation law to some degree; however, incorporation matters remain largely a state decision, with no federal incorporation statute for accountants in existence.

The resolution of corporate policy through adherence to state law is not always without incident as conflicts arise among state mandates. Your professional accounting corporation is more than a creature of state law; it is also a professional business corporation engaged in the practice of a particular profession, specifically accounting. As such, it will be subject to the mandates of your state's professional corporation law, business corporation law, and laws regulating the accounting profession. It is therefore clear that there exist many opportunities for conflict among these three bodies of law. To remedy this situation, some states have repealed or amended inconsistent regulatory or licensing statutes; however, the majority of jurisdictions have included in their professional corporation laws provisions making the professional corporation law supreme by mandating that other laws are restricted to the extent that they are inconsistent with the professional corporation law. For those matters over which you are able to exercise some degree of control, a well-planned course of action is recommended, since the accounting corporation that resolves questions before they grow into practice management problems will surely have the competitive edge.

## ACCOUNTANT AND ATTORNEY: A TEAM FOR SUCCESS

The attorney's role in the choice and creation of your practice organization ensures your awareness not only of legal rights and obligations but also of the legality and enforceability of your organizational documents. Your lawyer can also assist in periodic reviews of your agreements so that appropriate revisions and amendments are made to reflect changes in laws, regulations, court decisions, and circumstances.

When you begin the process of organizing your practice, whether your choice be the partnership or professional corporation, schedule a meeting, to be attended by the principals of your firm and lawyer, so that all parties can present their proposals. If possible, select an attorney who is both familiar with your firm and experienced in partnership and corporate law. Be prepared to encounter some short-term conflicts among participants during this introductory stage; however, remain committed and aware of the long-term benefits to you and your firm. Functioning in this manner can provide all participants with a sense of certainty that nothing has been said to the attorney or to other firm members that may be detrimental to their interests. If necessary, it can also serve as a perfect opportunity to provide counsel with a complete understanding of the firm and the relationships among its members. Throughout your organizational process, remember that the success of any partnership or professional corporation will be determined by the skill and effort that went into its formation.

Two questions that frequently confront accountants while working with their attorney in these matters are the manner in which attorneys become proficient in this specialty of law and the extent of the attorney's involvement. In most cases, a lawyer's first exposure to partnership and corporation law can be traced to a law school curriculum, with expertise resulting from post-law school specialization. Your attorney's involvement can range from the far-reaching role of participating in the entire process to the more restricted one of documenting the partners' intentions. The recommended approach for you, the accountant, and the one made possible by this book, is to take advantage of your technical expertise, practical experience, and inherent knowledge of your firm's characteristics and prepare an outline of your agreement(s). This document(s) can then be reviewed and completed by your attorney. As an expert in the legal enforceability of organizational documents, your attorney can advise you of any necessary additions, deletions, or revisions that must be made. After further discussion among the members of your firm, the draft can be formalized to become a legally enforceable document. Since all firms are unique, it is you, as a practitioner and professional, who knows how the interests of your firm are best represented. Conversely, your attorney, as a skilled professional trained in this specialty, is adept at drafting agreements that conform to the law. Acting in concert with these guidelines results in the joining of two technical experts and the creation of complete, binding agreements that manifest your precise intentions.

You cannot underestimate your own involvement in this process, since the definitive partnership agreement and incorporation documents reflect your personal management style and are written in a fashion that is readily understood by all members of your firm. Entrusting this responsibility solely to your attorney may result in an incomplete agreement overwrought with legalisms that may be misunderstood. Assuming this responsibility yourself may result in unenforceable or incomplete agreements. These exact sentiments were considered when the model provisions included in this book were drafted. By conforming to these principles, you can achieve complete, enforceable organizational documents as well as savings in legal expenses.

# CONCLUSION

The message conveyed by this book is that all firms should practice under well-drafted organizational documents that reflect their individual management philosophy and that are broad enough to accommodate change. Regardless of the form, a successful practice is best achieved through a complete, enforceable partnership agreement or corporate documents. Making these agreements an integral part of your practice not only enables you to maintain your current level of success, but also allows you to prosper and take advantage of the growing professional opportunities now becoming available in the field of accounting.

*The illustrative material below has been included for informational purposes only. Practitioners who feel that any of this material would be useful in their own agreements are advised to consult legal counsel for specific advice on the appropriateness and effect of such use.*

# Articles of Incorporation
# of

*[Name of Firm]*

KNOW ALL MEN BY THESE PRESENTS, that the undersigned natural person, being more than 18 years of age, acting as the Incorporator in order to organize and establish a corporation under the _____ Code does hereby adopt the following Articles of Incorporation, to wit:

## I. NAME

The name of the Corporation is: _____.

## II. REGISTERED OFFICE AND REGISTERED AGENT

The initial Registered Office for the Corporation is _____.
The initial Registered Agent at such address is _____.

## III. PURPOSES

The objects and purposes for which this Corporation is organized and the nature of the business to be carried on by it are as follows:

1.  To carry on the practice of accountancy and such other activities as may from time to time be specifically found by the Board to be activities suitable and proper to be performed by certified public accountants in accordance with the standards of professional conduct promulgated in the State of _____.

*FOR DISCUSSION PURPOSES ONLY*

2.  To impose restrictions upon the transfer of its own shares in compliance with limitations imposed by law and upon such terms as its Board of Directors may direct.

3.  In general, to carry on any business or activity in connection with the foregoing and to have and exercise all of the powers and rights conferred by the laws of the State of _____ upon professional corporations formed under such laws.

# IV. CAPITAL STOCK

**Section 1. Authorized Shares.**   The total number of shares which this Corporation is authorized to issue is _____ (____) shares of common stock of no par value.

**Section 2. Voting Rights of Shareholders.**  Each holder of the common stock shall be entitled to one vote for each share of stock recorded in his name on the books of the Corporation. Cumulative voting shall not be permitted.

**Section 3. Consideration for Shares.**   Shares without a par value shall be issued for such consideration as shall be fixed from time to time by the Board of Directors. The judgment of the Board of Directors as to the value of the consideration received in full or partial payment for shares shall be conclusive. When shares are issued upon payment of the consideration fixed by the Board of Directors, such shares shall be deemed to be fully paid stock and shall be nonassessable.

**Section 4. Denial of Preemptive Rights.**  The Corporation's shareholders are denied the preemptive right to purchase its shares. Therefore, the Corporation need not offer to sell a pro rata proportion of its stock or securities convertible into stock to its shareholders before selling, or offering to sell, any additional shares of its stock or any stocks, bonds, debentures, or other securities convertible into its stock.

**Section 5. Stock Transfer Restrictions.**  The Corporation shall have the right to impose restrictions on the transfer of all or any part of its shares prior to the issuance thereof and may become a party to agreements entered into by any of its shareholders restricting transfer or encumbrance of any of its shares or subjecting any of its shares to repurchase or resale obligations.

# V. MANAGEMENT

For the management of the business, for the conduct of the affairs of the Corporation, and for the further definition, limitation, and regulation of the powers of the Corporation, its directors and shareholders, it is further provided:

**Section 1. Size of Board.** Except as provided herein, the number of directors shall be established in the manner provided by the Bylaws; the number of directors constituting the initial Board of Directors of the Corporation is _____. The names and addresses of the persons who are to serve as the initial directors are as follows:

_____    _____
                            _____
_____    _____
                            _____

**Section 2. Powers of Board.** The Board of Directors may exercise all such powers and do all such acts and things as may be exercised or done by the Corporation or as are appropriate to the management of the business and the conduct of the affairs of the Corporation, subject, nevertheless, to the provisions of the laws of the State of _____, of these Articles of Incorporation, and of the Bylaws of the Corporation.

**Section 3. Interested Directors.** No contract or transaction between this Corporation and one or more of its directors, or between this Corporation and any other corporation, firm, association, or other entity in which one or more of the Corporation's directors or officers are directors or officers or are financially interested, shall be void or voidable solely for that reason or solely because the director or officer is present at or participates in the meeting of the Board of Directors or a committee thereof which authorizes, approves, or ratifies such contract or transaction, or solely because their votes are counted for such purpose, provided that (i) the material facts as to the relationship or interest of such director and as to the contract or transaction shall have been disclosed to or known by the Board of Directors or committee which in good faith authorizes, approves, or ratifies the contract or transaction by a vote or consent sufficient for the purpose without counting the vote or consent of such interested directors, even though the disinterested directors constitute less than a quorum, or (ii) said material facts shall have been disclosed to or known by the shareholders entitled to vote on the contract or transaction, and they authorize, approve, or ratify the contract or transaction in good faith by a vote of said share-holders, or (iii) the contract or transaction was fair as to the Corporation.

Common or interested directors may be counted in determining the presence of a quorum at a meeting of the Board of Directors or a committee thereof which authorizes, approves, or ratifies such contract or transaction.

**Section 4. Indemnification.** The Corporation shall indemnify its Officers and Directors to the maximum extent allowed by law so long as such indemnification does not cause the Corporation's liabilities to exceed its assets as determined in accordance with generally accepted accounting principles. For purposes of this Section, the term "Director" means an individual who is or was a director of the Corporation and an individual who, while a director of the Corporation, is or was serving at the Corporation's request as a director, officer, partner, trustee, employee, or agent of any other foreign or domestic corporation or of any partnership, joint venture, trust, other enterprise, or employee benefit plan. A director shall be consid-ered to be serving an employee benefit plan at the Corporation's request if his duties to the Corporation also impose duties on, or otherwise involve services by him to, the plan or to participants in or beneficiaries of the plan. "Director" includes, unless the context otherwise requires, the estate or personal representative of a director.

**Section 5. Personal Liability.**

*A.* Except as otherwise provided by law, a director shall not be personally liable to the Corporation or to its shareholders for monetary damages for breach of fiduciary duty as a director. Notwithstanding the immediately preceding sentence, nothing in this Subsection A shall eliminate or limit the liability of a director of the Corporation or its shareholders for monetary damages for (i) any breach of the director's duty of loyalty to the Corpora-tion or to its shareholders, (ii) acts or omissions not in good faith or which involve intentional misconduct or a knowing violation of law, (iii) acts specified in Section _____ of the _____ Corporation Code, or (iv) any transaction from which the director derived an improper personal benefit.

*FOR DISCUSSION PURPOSES ONLY*

*B.* Except as otherwise provided by law, no officer or director shall be personally liable for any injury to person or property arising out of a tort committed by an employee unless such officer or director was personally involved in the situation giving rise to the litigation, or unless the officer or director committed a criminal offense. The protection afforded by this Subsection B shall not restrict other common law protections and rights that an officer or director may have or affect the elimination of personal liability of a director to the Corporation or to its shareholders for monetary damages for breach of fiduciary duty as a director under Subsection A of this Section 5.

## VI. AMENDMENT OF ARTICLES

The provisions of these Articles of Incorporation may be amended, altered, or repealed from time to time in the manner prescribed by the laws of the State of _____, with a two-thirds (2/3) vote of the shareholders entitled to vote thereon, unless any class of shares is entitled to vote thereon as a class, in which event the proposed amendment shall be adopted upon receiving the affirmative vote of the holders of two-thirds (2/3) of the shares of said class and of the total shares entitled to vote thereon. All rights herein conferred on the directors, officers, and shareholders are granted and subject to this reservation.

## VII. PLACE OF MEETING; CORPORATE BOOKS

Subject to the laws of the State of _____, the shareholders and the directors shall have power to hold their meetings, and the directors shall have power to have an office or offices and to maintain the books of the Corporation outside the State of _____, at such place or places as may from time to time be designated in the Bylaws or by appropriate resolution.

## VIII. SHAREHOLDER QUALIFICATIONS AND LIMITATIONS

**Section 1. Qualifications of Shareholders.** All shareholders of this Corporation shall be persons who must be certified public accountants or registered accountants in good standing in the State of _____ and

*FOR DISCUSSION PURPOSES ONLY*

shall at all times own their shares in their own right. They shall be individuals who, except for illness, accident, and time spent in the armed services, on vacations, and on leaves of absence not to exceed one (1) year, are actively engaged in the practice of accounting in the offices of the Corporation in _____ .

**Section 2. Loss of Qualifications.** Shareholders who cease to be, or for any reason are ineligible to be, shareholders shall dispose of all of their shares forthwith, either to this Corporation or to any person having the qualifications of a shareholder under this Article.

**Section 3. Qualifications of Officers and Directors.** Notwithstanding anything to the contrary herein provided, the President shall be a shareholder and director of this Corporation, and to the extent possible, all other directors and officers shall be persons having the qualifications of a shareholder under this Article. Lay directors and officers shall not exercise any authority whatsoever over professional matters.

**Section 4. Agreement of Shareholders.** The acquisition by a shareholder of stock in this Corporation signifies the shareholder's agreement to the provisions of Article IX below.

# IX. LIMITED LIABILITY OF SHAREHOLDERS

All shareholders of this Corporation shall be, and said shareholders agree to be, jointly and severally liable for all acts, errors, and omissions of the employees of the Corporation with respect to performance of professional services only except during periods of time when either (i) each person who holds a certificate to practice public accounting as a certified public accountant or as a registered accountant who is a shareholder, or any employee of the Corporation, has a professional liability policy insuring himself and all other employees who act at his direction, or (ii) this Corporation maintains in good standing professional liability insurance, which insurance shall meet the minimum standards set forth in Sections _____ of _____ Revised Statutes, as currently enacted and as subsequently amended.

*FOR DISCUSSION PURPOSES ONLY*

# X. DATA RESPECTING INCORPORATOR

The name and address of the Incorporator of the Corporation, a natural person, is _____.

Executed this _____ day of _____, 19XX.

STATE OF _____)
                     ) ss.
COUNTY OF _____)

I, _____, the undersigned Notary Public duly commissioned to take acknowledgments and administer oaths in the State of _____, do hereby certify that on this _____ day of _____, 19XX, _____ personally appeared before me, who, being first duly sworn, declared that [he/she] is the only Incorporator referred to in Article VIII of the foregoing Articles of Incorporation, and that [he/she] signed these Articles as such and that the statements contained therein are true.

Witness my hand and official seal.

My Commission Expires: _____

(SEAL)                              _____
                                           Notary Public

*FOR DISCUSSION PURPOSES ONLY*

*The illustrative material below has been included for informational purposes only. Practitioners who feel that any of this material would be useful in their own agreements are advised to consult legal counsel for specific advice on the appropriateness and effect of such use.*

# Bylaws
# of

[*Name of Firm*]

## I. OFFICE

**Section 1. Principal Office.** The initial principal office of the Corporation shall be located at _____. This office may be changed and the Corporation may also have offices at such other places, both within and without the State of _____, as the Board of Directors may determine or as the affairs of the Corporation may require from time to time.

**Section 2. Registered Office.** The initial registered office of the Corporation in the State of _____ shall be at _____.

## II. SHAREHOLDERS' MEETINGS

**Section 1. Annual Meetings.**

*A. Time and Place.* The annual meeting of the Shareholders of the Corporation, commencing with the year of incorporation, shall be held at the principal office of the Corporation in the State of _____ or at such other place within or without the State of _____ as may be determined by the Board of Directors and as may be designated in the notice of such meeting. The meeting shall be held on the forty-fifth (45th) day following the end of the Corporation's fiscal year. If said day is a legal holiday, the meeting shall be held on the next succeeding day that is not a legal holiday.

*B. Purpose of Meeting.* The business to be transacted at such meeting shall be the election of Directors and such other business as shall be properly brought before the meeting.

*FOR DISCUSSION PURPOSES ONLY*

*C. Alternate Election Date.* If the election of Directors shall not be held on the day designated for any annual meeting, or at any adjournment of such meeting, the Board of Directors shall call a special meeting of the Shareholders as soon as conveniently possible thereafter. At such meeting, the election of Directors shall take place, and such election and any other business transacted thereat shall have the same force and effect as if conducted at an annual meeting duly called and held.

*D. Notice.* No change in the time or place for the meeting for the election of Directors shall be made within ten (10) days preceding the day on which the election is to be held. Written notice of any such change shall be given each Shareholder at least ten (10) days before the election is held, either in person or by letter mailed to him at the address last shown on the books of the Corporation.

**Section 2. Special Meetings.**   Special meetings of the Shareholders may be called for any purpose or purposes, unless otherwise prohibited by statute or by the Articles of Incorporation, by the Chairman of the Board, if any, or the President, and shall be called by the President or Secretary at the request in writing of Shareholders owning not less than one-tenth (1/10) of all of the shares of the capital stock of the Corporation issued and outstanding and entitled to vote. Such request shall state the purpose or purposes of the proposed meeting.

**Section 3. Notice and Purpose of Meetings; Waiver.**   Each Shareholder of record entitled to vote at any meeting shall be given, in person or by mail, or by prepaid telegram, written or printed notice of the purpose or purposes and the time and place of every meeting of Shareholders. Except as provided by the _____ Corporation Code, such notice shall be mailed not less than ten (10) days before the meeting nor more than fifty (50) days prior to the meeting; provided, however, that at least thirty (30) days' notice shall be given of all meetings at which it is proposed that the number of authorized shares be increased. No publication of the notice of the meeting shall be required. A Shareholder may waive the notice of meeting by attendance, either in person or by proxy, at the meeting or by so stating in writing, either before or after such meeting. Attendance at a meeting for the express purpose of objecting that the meeting was not lawfully called or convened shall not, however, constitute a waiver of notice if such objection is made at the beginning of the meeting. When a meeting is adjourned to another time or place, notice need not be given of the adjourned meeting if the time and place thereof are announced at the meeting at which the adjournment is taken. At the adjourned meeting the Corporation may transact any business which might have been transacted at the original meeting. If the adjournment is for more than thirty (30) days, or if after the adjournment a new record date is fixed for the adjourned meeting, a notice of the adjourned meeting shall be given to each Shareholder of record entitled to vote at the meeting.

**Section 4. Quorum.** Except as otherwise provided by law, a quorum at all meetings of Shareholders shall consist of the holders of record of a majority of the shares entitled to vote thereat, present in person or by proxy. If a quorum is not represented at any meeting of the Shareholders, such meeting may be adjourned for a period not to exceed sixty (60) days at any one adjournment.

**Section 5. Closing of Transfer Books; Record Date.** In order to determine the holders of record of the Corporation's stock who are entitled to receive notice of meetings, to vote at a meeting or on an adjournment thereof, and to receive payment of any dividend, or to make a determination of the Shareholders of record for any other proper purpose, the Board of Directors of the Corporation may order that its Stock Transfer Books be closed for a period not to exceed fifty (50) days. If the purpose of such closing is to determine who is entitled to notice of a meeting and to vote at such meeting, the Stock Transfer Books shall be closed for at least ten (10) days immediately preceding such meeting.

*A. Record Date.* In lieu of closing the Stock Transfer Books, the Board of Directors may fix a date as the record date for such determination of Shareholders. Such date shall be no more than fifty (50) days prior to the date of the action that requires such determination, nor, in the case of a Shareholders' meeting, shall it be less than ten (10) days in advance of such meeting.

*B. Alternate Record Date.* If the Stock Transfer Books are not closed and no record date is fixed for such determination of the Shareholders of record, the date on which notice of the meeting is mailed, or on which the resolution of the Board of Directors declaring a dividend is adopted, as the case may be, shall be the record date for such determination of Shareholders.

*C. Adjournment.* When a determination of Shareholders entitled to vote at any meeting has been made as provided in this Section, such determination shall apply to any adjournment of such meeting, except when the determination has been made by the closing of the Stock Transfer Books and the stated period of closing has expired.

### Section 6. Presiding Officer; Order of Business.

A. *Presiding Officer.* Meetings of the Shareholders shall be presided over by the Chairman of the Board. If he is not present, or if there is none, they shall be presided over by the President or if he is not present or if there is none, by a Vice President or, if he is not present or if there is none, by a person chosen by the Board of Directors or, if no such person is present or has been chosen, by a Chairman to be chosen by Shareholders who own a majority of the shares of the capital stock of the Corporation issued and outstanding and are entitled to vote at the meeting and are present in person or represented by proxy. The Secretary of the Corporation or, if he is not present, an Assistant Secretary or, if he is not present, a person chosen by the Board of Directors shall act as Secretary at meetings of Shareholders; if no such person is present or has been chosen, the Shareholders who own a majority of the shares of capital stock of the Corporation issued and outstanding and are entitled to vote at the meeting and are present in person or represented by proxy shall choose any person present to act as Secretary of the meeting.

B. *Order of Business.* The following order of business, unless otherwise determined at the meeting, shall be observed as far as practicable and consistent with the purposes of the meeting:

1. Calling of the meeting to Order
2. Presentation of proof of mailing of the notice of the meeting and, if the meeting is a special meeting, the call thereof
3. Presentation of proxies
4. Announcement that a quorum is present
5. Reading and approval of the minutes of the previous meeting
6. Reports, if any, of Officers
7. Election of Directors, if the meeting is an annual meeting or a meeting is called for that purpose
8. Consideration of the specific purpose or purposes, other than the election of Directors, for which the meeting has been called, if the meeting is a special meeting

*FOR DISCUSSION PURPOSES ONLY*

9. Transaction of such other business as may properly come before the meeting

10. Adjournment

**Section 7. Voting.** At every meeting of the Shareholders, each Shareholder of the Corporation entitled to vote at such meeting shall have, as to each matter submitted to a vote, one vote in person or by proxy for each share of stock having voting rights registered in his name on the books of the Corporation. If a share is registered in the names of two or more persons as fiduciaries, partners, tenants in common, joint tenants, tenants by entirety, or otherwise, then voting with respect to said share shall be in the manner provided by the _____ Corporation Code. A Shareholder may vote his shares through a proxy appointed by a written instrument signed by the Shareholder or by his duly authorized attorney-in-fact which is delivered to the Secretary of the meeting. No proxy shall be valid after eleven (11) months from the date of its execution unless a longer period is expressly provided therein.

**Section 8. Manner of Acting.** All elections shall be determined by a plurality vote, and except as otherwise provided by law or the Articles of Incorporation, all other matters shall be determined by a vote of a majority of the shares present in person or represented by proxy and voting on such other matters.

**Section 9. Record of Shareholders.** The Officer in charge of the stock ledger of the Corporation or the transfer agent shall prepare and make, at least ten (10) days before every meeting of Shareholders, a complete list of the Shareholders entitled to vote at the meeting, arranged in alphabetical order and showing the address and the number of shares registered in the name of each Shareholder. Such list shall be open to the examination of any Shareholder, for any purpose germane to the meeting, during ordinary business hours, for a period of at least ten (10) days prior to the meeting, at the principal office of the Corporation. The list shall also be produced and kept at the place of the meeting during the whole time thereof and may be inspected by any Shareholder who is present in person thereat.

*A. Shareholder Determination.* The original Stock Transfer Books shall be prima facie evidence of the Shareholders' entitlement to examine such record or to vote at any meeting of the Shareholders.

*FOR DISCUSSION PURPOSES ONLY*

*B. Validity of Shareholder Meetings.* Failure to comply with the requirements of this Section shall not affect the validity of any action taken at such meeting of the Shareholders.

**Section 10. Action by Consent.**   Any action required or permitted by law or the Articles of Incorporation to be taken at any meeting of Shareholders may be taken without a meeting, without prior notice, and without a vote, if one or more written consents setting forth the action so taken shall be signed by all of the holders of the outstanding stock having the right to vote thereon. Such written consent(s) shall be filed with the minutes of the meeting of Shareholders. Any action taken by consent is effective when all Shareholders entitled to vote have signed the consent, unless the consent specifies a different effective date. The record date for determining Shareholders entitled to take action without a meeting is the date the first Shareholder signs the consent. A written consent taken in accordance with this Section has the same force and effect as a unanimous vote of the Shareholders.

# III. DIRECTORS

**Section 1. General Powers, Number, and Tenure.**   The business of the Corporation shall be managed by its Board of Directors, which may exercise all powers of the Corporation and perform all lawful acts that are not by law, the Articles of Incorporation, or these Bylaws directed or required to be exercised or performed by the Shareholders. The number of Directors shall be determined by the Board of Directors. If no such determination is made, or regardless of a previous determination if no redetermination is made after a change in the number of Shareholders, the number of Directors shall be three (3) except and unless there is a lesser number of Shareholders of record, in which case that number shall be the number of Directors. No decrease in the number of Directors shall have the effect of shortening the term of any incumbent Director. The Directors shall be elected at the annual meeting of the Shareholders, except as provided in Section 2 of this Article, and each Director elected shall hold office until his successor is elected and shall qualify. Directors need not be Shareholders.

**Section 2. Vacancies.**   If any vacancies occur in the Board of Directors, or if any new Directorships are created, they may be filled by a majority of the Directors then in office, although such majority constitutes less than a quorum, or by a sole remaining Director. Each Director so chosen shall hold office until the next annual meeting of Shareholders and until his successor is duly elected and shall qualify. If there are no Directors in office, any Officer or Shareholder may call a special meeting of Shareholders in accordance with the provisions of the Certificate of Incorporation or these Bylaws, at which meeting such vacancies shall be filled.

**Section 3. Quorum.**    A majority of Directors in office shall be necessary to constitute a quorum for the transaction of business. If at any meeting of the Board of Directors there shall be less than a quorum present, a majority of those present may adjourn the meeting without further notice, from time to time, until a quorum shall have been obtained.

**Section 4. Meetings.**

*A. Regular Meetings.* Regular meetings of the Board of Directors may be held either within or without the State of _____. Regular meetings of the Board of Directors shall be held at such times as are fixed from time to time by resolution of the Board of Directors. The annual meeting of each newly elected Board of Directors shall be held without notice immediately following the annual meeting of the Shareholders. Notice need not be given of regular meetings of the Board of Directors held at times fixed by resolution of the Board of Directors, nor of the business to be transacted at such meeting.

*B. Special Meetings.* Special meetings of the Board of Directors may be called by the President on twenty-four (24) hours' notice to each Director, given personally or by mail, or by telephone or telegraph, which notice shall state the time, place (as hereinabove provided), and purpose of the meeting. Special meetings of the Board of Directors shall be called by the President or Secretary, in like manner and on like notice, on the written request of at least a majority of the Directors then in office. By attending or participating in a special meeting, a Director waives any required notice of such meeting unless the Director, at the beginning of the meeting, objects to the holding of the meeting or the transacting of business at the meeting.

*C. Telephonic Meetings.* Members of the Board of Directors or of any committee designated by the Board of Directors may participate in a meeting of the Board of Directors or committee thereof by means of a conference telephone call or by similar means of communication by which all persons participating in the meeting can hear one another at the same time. Such participation shall constitute presence in person at the meeting.

*FOR DISCUSSION PURPOSES ONLY*

### Section 5. Removal or Resignation.

*A. Removal.* Except as otherwise provided by law or the Articles of Incorporation, at any meeting of Shareholders, any Director or Directors may be removed from office, without assignment of any reason therefor, by a majority vote of the shares or class of shares, as the case may be, which elected the Director or Directors to be removed. When any Director or Directors are removed, new Directors may be elected at the same meeting of Shareholders for the unexpired term of the Director or Directors removed. If the Shareholders fail to elect persons to fill the unexpired term or terms of the Director or Directors removed, such unexpired term or terms shall be considered a vacancy or vacancies on the Board of Directors to be filled by the remaining Directors.

*B. Resignation.* Any Director may resign at any time by giving written notice to the Board of Directors, the Chairman of the Board, if any, or the President or Secretary of the Corporation. Unless otherwise specified in such written notice, a resignation shall take effect upon delivery thereof to the Board of Directors or the designated Officer. It shall not be necessary for a resignation to be accepted before it becomes effective.

### Section 6. Compensation.

Directors and members of any committee of the Board of Directors shall be entitled to such reasonable compensation for their services as Directors and members of any such committee as shall be fixed from time to time by resolution of the Board of Directors, and shall also be entitled to reimbursement for any reasonable expenses incurred in attending such meetings. The compensation of Directors may be on such basis as is determined in the resolution of the Board of Directors. Any Director receiving compensation under these provisions shall not be barred from serving the Corporation in any other capacity and receiving reasonable compensation for such other services.

### Section 7. Manner of Acting.

*A. One Vote Per Director.* At all meetings of the Board of Directors, each Director present shall have one (1) vote, irrespective of the number of shares of stock, if any, which he may hold.

*B. Percent of Quorum.* Except as otherwise provided by statute, by the Articles of Incorporation, or by these Bylaws, the action of a majority of the Directors present at any meeting at which a quorum is present shall be the act of the Board of Directors. If a quorum is not present at any meeting of the Board of Directors, the Directors present may adjourn the meeting from time to time, without notice, other than announcement at the meeting at which the adjournment is taken, until a quorum shall be present.

*C. Manifestation of Dissent.* A Director of the Corporation who is present at a meeting of the Board of Directors at which action on any corporate matter is taken shall be presumed to have assented to the action taken, unless he contemporaneously requests that his dissent be entered in the Minutes of the meeting, or he shall give a written dissent to such action to the presiding officer of the meeting before its adjournment or to the Secretary of the Corporation immediately after the adjournment of the meeting. Such right to dissent shall not apply to a Director who voted in favor of such action.

**Section 8. Action by Consent.** Any action required or permitted to be taken at any meeting of Directors may be taken without a meeting if a written consent to such action is signed by all members of the Board of Directors and such written consent is filed with the minutes of its proceedings. Such action is effective when all Directors have signed the consent, unless the consent specifies a different effective date. Such consent has the same force and effect as a unanimous vote of the Directors.

# IV. COMMITTEES

**Section 1. Executive Committee.** The Board of Directors, by resolution adopted by a majority of the whole Board, may appoint an Executive Committee consisting of one (1) or more Directors, one (1) of whom shall be designated as Chairman of the Executive Committee. Each member of the Executive Committee shall continue as a member thereof until the expiration of his term as a Director or his earlier resignation, unless sooner removed as a member or as a Director.

**Section 2. Powers.** The Executive Committee shall have and may exercise those rights, powers, and authority of the Board of Directors as may from time to time be granted to it by the Board of Directors, to the extent permitted by law, and may authorize the seal of the Corporation to be affixed to all papers that may require it.

**Section 3. Procedure and Meetings.** The Executive Committee shall fix its own rules of procedure and shall meet at such times and at such place or places as may be provided by such rules or as the members of the Executive Committee shall fix. The Executive Committee shall keep regular minutes of its meetings, which it shall deliver to the Board of Directors from time to time. The Chairman of the Executive Committee or, in his absence, a member of the Executive Committee chosen by majority of the members present shall preside at meetings of the Executive Committee, and another member chosen by the Executive Committee shall act as Secretary of the Executive Committee.

**Section 4. Quorum.**   A majority of the Executive Committee shall constitute a quorum for the transaction of its business, and the affirmative vote of a majority of its members present at any meeting at which there is a quorum shall be required for any action of the Executive Committee, provided, however, that when an Executive Committee of one (1) member is authorized under the provisions of Section 1 of this Article, that one (1) member shall constitute a quorum.

**Section 5. Other Committees.**   The Board of Directors, by resolution adopted by a majority of the whole Board, may appoint such other committee or committees as it shall deem advisable and with such rights, powers, and authority as it shall prescribe. Each such committee shall consist of one (1) or more Directors.

**Section 6. Committee Changes.**   The Board of Directors shall have the power at any time to fill vacancies in, to change the membership of, and to discharge any committee.

**Section 7. Compensation.**   Members of any committee shall be entitled to such compensation for their services as members of the committee and to such reimbursement for any reasonable expenses incurred in attending committee meetings as may, from time to time, be fixed by the Board of Directors. Any committee member receiving compensation under these provisions shall not be barred from serving the Corporation in any other capacity and from receiving compensation and reimbursement of reasonable expenses for such other services.

**Section 8. Action by Consent.**   Any action required or permitted to be taken at any meeting of a committee of the Board of Directors may be taken without a meeting if a written consent to such action is signed by all members of the committee and such written consent is filed with the minutes of its proceedings. Such action is effective when all committee members have signed the consent, unless the consent specifies a different effective date. Such consent has the same force and effect as a unanimous vote of the members.

**Section 9. Telephonic Meetings.**   One or more members of any committee designated by the Board of Directors may participate in a meeting of such committee by means of a conference telephone call or similar communications equipment by means of which all persons participating in the meeting can hear one another at the same time. Such participation shall constitute presence in person at the meeting.

# V. OFFICERS

**Section 1. Designations.**   The Officers of the Corporation shall be chosen by the Board of Directors. The Board of Directors may choose a Chairman of the Board, a President, a Vice President or Vice Presidents, a Secretary, a Treasurer, one or more Assistant Secretaries and/or Assistant Treasurers, and other officers and agents that it shall deem necessary or appropriate. All Officers of the Corporation shall exercise the powers and perform the duties that shall from time to time be determined by the Board of Directors. Any number of offices may be held by the same person, unless the Certificate of Incorporation or these Bylaws provide otherwise.

**Section 2. Term of, and Removal From, Office.**   At its first regular meeting after each annual meeting of Shareholders, the Board of Directors shall choose a President, a Secretary, and a Treasurer. It may also choose a Chairman of the Board, a Vice President or Vice Presidents, one or more Assistant Secretaries and/or Assistant Treasurers, and such other officers and agents as it shall deem necessary or appropriate. Each Officer of the Corporation shall hold office until his successor is chosen and qualified. Any Officer elected or appointed by the Board of Directors may be removed, with or without cause, at any time by the affirmative vote of a majority of the Directors then in office. Removal from office, however, shall not prejudice the contract rights, if any, of the person removed. Any vacancy occurring in any office of the Corporation may be filled for the unexpired portion of the term by the Board of Directors.

**Section 3. Compensation.**   The salaries of all Officers of the Corporation shall be fixed from time to time by the Board of Directors, and no Officer shall be prevented from receiving a salary because he is also a Director of the Corporation.

**Section 4.  The Chairman of the Board.**   The Chairman of the Board, if any, shall be an Officer of the Corporation and, subject to the direction of the Board of Directors, shall perform such executive, supervisory, and management functions and duties as may be assigned to him from time to time by the Board of Directors. He shall, if present, preside at all meetings of Shareholders and of the Board of Directors.

**Section 5.  The President.**

*A.  Duties.* The President shall be the Chief Executive Officer of the Corporation and, subject to the direction of the Board of Directors, shall have general charge of the business affairs and property of the Corporation and general supervision over its other officers and agents. In general, he shall perform all duties incident to the office of President and shall see that all orders and resolutions of the Board of Directors are carried into effect. In addition to and not in limitation of the foregoing, the President shall be empowered to authorize any change of the registered office or registered agent, or both, of the Corporation in the State of _____ .

*B.  Voting Corporate Securities.* Unless otherwise prescribed by the Board of Directors, the President shall have full power and authority to attend, act, and vote on behalf of the Corporation at any meeting of the security holders of other corporations in which the Corporation may hold securities. At any such meeting, the President shall possess and may exercise any and all rights and powers incident to the ownership of such securities that the Corporation might have possessed and exercised if it had been present. The Board of Directors may from time to time confer like powers upon any other person or persons.

**Section 6.  The Vice President.**   The Vice President, if any, or, in the event there be more than one, the Vice Presidents in the order designated or, in the absence of any designation, in the order of their election shall, in the absence of the President or in the event of his disability, perform the duties and exercise the powers of the President and shall generally assist the President and perform such other duties and have such other powers as may from time to time be prescribed by the Board of Directors.

*FOR DISCUSSION PURPOSES ONLY*

**Section 7. The Secretary.** The Secretary shall attend all meetings of the Board of Directors and the Shareholders and record all votes and the proceedings of the meetings in a book to be kept for that purpose. He shall perform like duties for the Executive Committee or other committees, if required. He shall give, or cause to be given, notice of all meetings of Shareholders and special meetings of the Board of Directors and shall perform such other duties as may from time to time be prescribed by the Board of Directors, the Chairman of the Board, or the President, under whose supervision he shall act. He shall have custody of the seal of the Corporation, and he, or an Assistant Secretary, shall have authority to affix it to any instrument requiring it, and when so affixed, the seal may be attested by his signature or by the signature of the Assistant Secretary. The Board of Directors may give general authority to any other Officer to affix the seal of the Corporation and to attest the affixing thereof by his signature.

**Section 8. The Assistant Secretary.** The Assistant Secretary, if any, or, in the event there be more than one, the Assistant Secretaries in the order designated or, in the absence of any designation, in the order of their election shall, in the absence of the Secretary or in the event of his disability, perform the duties and exercise the powers of the Secretary and shall perform such other duties and have such other powers as may from time to time be prescribed by the Board of Directors.

**Section 9. The Treasurer.** The Treasurer shall have the custody of the corporate funds and other valuable effects, including securities, and shall keep full and accurate accounts of receipts and disbursements in books belonging to the Corporation and shall deposit all monies and other valuable effects in the name and to the credit of the Corporation in such depositories as may from time to time be designated by the Board of Directors. He shall disburse the funds of the Corporation in accord with the orders of the Board of Directors, taking proper vouchers for such disbursements, and shall render to the Chairman of the Board, if any, the President, and the Board of Directors, whenever they may require it or at regular meetings of the Board, an account of all his transactions as Treasurer and the financial condition of the Corporation.

**Section 10. The Assistant Treasurer.** The Assistant Treasurer, if any, or, in the event there shall be more than one, the Assistant Treasurers in the order designated or, in the absence of any designation, in the order of their election shall, in the absence of the Treasurer or in the event of his disability,

*FOR DISCUSSION PURPOSES ONLY*

perform the duties and exercise the powers of the Treasurer and shall perform such other duties and have such other powers as may from time to time be prescribed by the Board of Directors.

# VI. CERTIFICATES OF STOCK

**Section 1. Form.** Except as provided in Section 3 below, the interest of each Shareholder in the Corporation shall be evidenced by certificates for shares of stock which shall certify the number of shares represented thereby. The certificates shall be in a form not inconsistent with the Articles of Incorporation or the laws of the State of _____, as the Board of Directors may from time to time prescribe.

A. *Certificates.* The certificates of stock shall be signed by the President or Vice President and Secretary or Assistant Secretary and shall be sealed with the seal of the Corporation.

B. *Transfers.* Transfers of shares of the capital stock of the Corporation shall be made only on the books of the Corporation upon authorization by the registered owner thereof or by his duly authorized attorney-in-fact.

C. *Owner of Certificates.* The person in whose name shares of stock stand on the books of the Corporation shall be deemed by the Corporation to be the owner thereof for all purposes. However, if any transfer of shares is made only for the purposes of furnishing collateral security, and such fact is made known to the Secretary of the Corporation or the Corporation's transfer clerk or transfer agent, the entry of the transfer shall record such fact.

**Section 2. Lost, Destroyed, or Stolen Certificates.** No certificate for shares of stock in the Corporation shall be issued in place of any certificate alleged to have been lost, destroyed, or stolen except on production of evidence, satisfactory to the Board of Directors of such loss, destruction, or theft, and, if the Board of Directors so requires, upon the furnishing of an indemnity bond in such amount with such terms and such surety as the Board of Directors may, in its discretion, require.

**Section 3. Shares Without Certificates.** The Board of Directors may authorize the issuance of any class or series of this Corporation's shares without certificates. Such authorization shall not affect shares already represented by certificates until they are surrendered to the Corporation. Within a reasonable time following the issue or transfer of shares without certificates, the Corporation shall send the Shareholder a complete written statement of the designations, preferences, limitations, and relative rights of the class together with all other information required by the _____ Corporation Code.

# VII. CORPORATION ACTIONS

The Board of Directors shall select banks, trust companies, or other depositories in which all funds of the Corporation not otherwise employed shall, from time to time, be deposited to the credit of the Corporation.

# VIII. CORPORATE SEAL

The Corporate Seal of the Corporation shall consist of two concentric circles. The name of the Corporation and the State of Incorporation shall be inscribed in the outer circle. In the center circle shall be inscribed the word "Seal."

# IX. AMENDMENT OF BYLAWS

**Section 1. By Shareholders.**   All Bylaws of the Corporation shall be subject to alteration or repeal by the Shareholders. New Bylaws may be made by the requisite vote of Shareholders, a quorum being present, provided that the notice or waiver of notice of such meeting shall have summarized or set forth in full therein the proposed amendment.

**Section 2. By Directors.**   The Board of Directors shall have power to make, adopt, alter, amend, and repeal, from time to time, Bylaws of the Corporation, provided, however, that the Shareholders entitled to vote with respect thereto, as provided in Section 1 above, may alter, amend, or repeal Bylaws made by the Board of Directors. Notwithstanding anything to the contrary herein provided, the Board of Directors shall not have power to change the quorum for meetings of Shareholders or of the Board of Directors or to change any provisions of these Bylaws with respect to the removal of Directors or the filling of vacancies in the Board of Directors resulting from the removal of Directors by the Shareholders. Moreover, if any Bylaw regulating an impending election of Directors is adopted, amended, or repealed by the Board of Directors, there shall be set forth, in the notice of the next meeting of Shareholders for the election of Directors, the Bylaw so adopted, amended, or repealed, together with a concise statement of the changes made.

# X. FISCAL YEAR

The fiscal year of the Corporation shall be fixed by the Board of Directors from time to time, subject to applicable law.

Ratified by the Board of Directors this the _____ day of _____ 19XX.

_____, CHAIRMAN

ATTEST BY:

_____, SECRETARY

*The illustrative material below has been included for informational purposes only. Practitioners who feel that any of this material would be useful in their own agreements are advised to consult legal counsel for specific advice on the appropriateness and effect of such use.*

# Employment Contract

THIS AGREEMENT is made as of _____, 19XX, by and between _____ ("Employee") and _____, a Professional Corporation ("Employer"), duly organized under the laws of the State of _____.

RECITALS

A. Employee is licensed and authorized to practice public accountancy in the State of _____.

B. Employee desires employment to practice public accountancy as an employee of Employer.

C. Employer desires to employ Employee under the terms and conditions of this Agreement.

NOW, THEREFORE, it is mutually agreed as follows:

**1. Employment.** Employer hereby employs Employee, and Employee hereby accepts employment by Employer on the terms and conditions set forth below.

**2. Services.** Employee agrees to devote substantially full time and attention to the practice of public accountancy for Employer. The expenditure by Employee of reasonable amounts of time for teaching, personal or outside business, and charitable and professional activities shall not be deemed a breach of this Agreement by Employee, provided such activities do not interfere with the services required to be rendered to Employer by Employee under this Agreement. During the term of this Agreement, Employee shall not, without Employer's express prior written consent, directly or indirectly render professional accounting services to or for any

*FOR DISCUSSION PURPOSES ONLY*

other person or firm for compensation or engage in any activity competitive with or adverse to Employer's business or practice, whether alone, as a partner, or as an officer, director, employee, or shareholder of any other corporation or as a trustee, a fiduciary, or other representative of any other entity. Employee may make passive and personal investments and conduct private business affairs not inconsistent with this Agreement without breach of this Agreement.

**3. Employer's Authority.** Subject to Employee's professional responsibilities, Employee agrees to observe and comply with Employer's rules and regulations as adopted by Employer's Board of Directors regarding performance of Employee's duties and to carry out and to perform orders, directions, and policies stated by Employer to Employee periodically, either orally or in writing. Employee agrees that in dealing with Employer's clients or prospective clients Employee will give no assurance in any form to such clients or prospective clients that Employee or any other particular employee of Employer will service a client, it being expressly understood that Employer shall have sole authority to determine which employees of Employer shall perform account services for any particular client of Employer.

**4. Term.** This Agreement shall be for a period of one (1) year, commencing on the _____ day of _____, 19XX, subject, however, to termination during such year, as provided herein. This Agreement shall be renewed automatically for succeeding periods of one (1) year each on the same terms and conditions as herein contained unless either the Employer, by its Board of Directors, or the Employee shall, at least forty-five (45) days prior to the expiration of any period, give written notice of his or its intention not to renew this Agreement.

**5. Compensation.**

A. Employer agrees to pay to Employee during the term of this Agreement a basic annual salary ("Basic Salary") in the amount of _____ dollars ($____), to be paid to Employee in equal semimonthly installments beginning on _____, 19XX, and payable on the fifteenth (15th) and last day of each month during the term of Employee's employment hereunder.

B. All fees and other compensation actually received by Employee for public accounting services performed by Employee for any person or entity or for acting as a director, trustee, or executor shall be the property of Employer and shall be remitted to Employer on receipt by Employee. All fees, honoraria, or other compensation received by Employee from teaching, lecturing, or publishing shall be the property of Employee. Any proceeds that Employee shall receive by virtue of disability insurance, disability benefits, or health or accident insurance shall be the property of Employee.

C. All compensation paid to Employee shall be subject to the customary withholding tax and other employment taxes as required with respect to compensation paid by a corporation to an employee.

**6. Vacation.** Employee shall be entitled to an annual vacation of _____ (____) weeks during the first three (3) fiscal years of employment and _____ (____) weeks during the fourth (4th) year and thereafter, without loss of compensation. The times for such vacation periods shall be those most convenient to Employer's business, as may be orally agreed to by Employer. Without Employer's consent, vacation time may not be accumulated but must be taken by Employee in the first year in which Employee is entitled to such vacation, or not at all.

**7. Termination.** Employee's employment with Employer shall be terminated if any of the following occurs:

A. Employee ceases to be an "eligible person" as defined in the Corporation Code or becomes a "disqualified person" as defined in the Corporation Code for a period of more than thirty (30) days.

B. Employer and Employee mutually agree in writing to termination.

C. Employee provides ninety (90) days' prior written notice.

D. Employee expires.

E. Employee fails to rectify a material breach of any of the terms, covenants, or conditions contained herein within thirty (30) days after written notice to Employee from Employer to cure such default.

F. At the option of Employer, whenever Employee becomes disabled and such disability lasts for a period in excess of ninety (90) days; provided, however, if such disability continues for a period of twelve (12) consecutive months, this Agreement shall thereupon terminate automatically. For purposes of this Agreement, "disability" shall be defined as Employee's

*FOR DISCUSSION PURPOSES ONLY*

inability, through physical or mental illness or other cause, to perform the majority of Employee's usual duties. Upon any Employee's disability, Employee shall be entitled to disability payments under Paragraph 9 of this Agreement.

G. At the option of Employer, for any reason whatsoever, without cause, the Employer and shareholders holding seventy-five percent (75%) of the outstanding Class B shares of Employer other than the Class B shares of Employer held by Employee vote to terminate.

H. Employee ceases, for any reason, to be a shareholder of Employer.

I. Employee offers Employee's shares of Employer for purchase by Employer pursuant to the terms of that certain Buy-Sell Agreement between the shareholders of Employer and Employer of even date herewith.

J. Employee attains the age of sixty-five (65) years ("Retirement") by the end of the fiscal year of Employer.

K. Dissolution of Employer occurs.

**8. Termination Payment: Other than Death or Permanent Disability.**

A. Except as provided in Paragraph 10, on termination of Employee's employment, for any reason other than retirement, death, or permanent disability, Employer shall pay Employee a Paragraph 8 Termination Payment equal to the product of (i) either one hundred seventy-five percent (175%) of the annual Basic Salary then being paid to Employee, if Employee does not engage in the active practice of public accountancy during the two (2) years following the date of termination in any of the following counties: _____; or one hundred percent (100%) of the annual Basic Salary then being paid to Employee, if Employee does engage in the active practice of public accountancy during the period of two (2) years following the date of termination in the aforementioned counties multiplied by (ii) the Paragraph 8 Vesting Factor for Employee at the time of such termination. The Paragraph 8 Termination Payment shall be due and payable, without interest, in twenty-four (24) equal monthly installments beginning on the first day of the month subsequent to the date of such termination.

B. The Paragraph 8 Vesting Factor for Employee shall be as follows: (i) If Employee shall have become a shareholder of Employer before calendar year 19XX, the Paragraph 8 Vesting Factor shall be equal to 1.00 at all times; (ii) if Employee shall have become a shareholder of Employer in any year after calendar year 19XX, the Paragraph 8 Vesting Factor shall be as follows: 0.0 during the period on and after the date Employee shall become a shareholder of Employer (the "Commencement Date") and before the date two (2) years after the Commencement Date; 0.25 during the period on and after the date two (2) years after the Commencement Date and before the date three (3) years after the Commencement Date; 0.50 during the period on and after the date three (3) years after the Commencement Date and before the date four (4) years after such Employee's Commencement Date; 0.75 during the period on and after the date four (4) years after the Commencement Date and before the date five (5) years after the Commencement Date; and equal to 1.00 at all times thereafter.

## 9. Termination Payment: Retirement, Death, or Permanent Disability.

A. Except as provided in Paragraph 10 below, on termination of Employee's employment because of retirement, death, or permanent disability, Employer shall pay Employee or Employee's estate, as the case may be, a Paragraph 9 Termination Payment equal to the product (i) two hundred fifty percent (250%) of the annual Basic Salary then being paid to Employee multiplied by (ii) the Paragraph 9 Vesting Factor for Employee on the date of such termination.

B. The Paragraph 9 Vesting Factor for Employee shall be as follows: (i) If Employee shall have become a shareholder of Employer before calendar year 19XX, the Paragraph 9 Vesting Factor shall be equal to 1.00 at all times; (ii) if Employee shall have become a shareholder of Employer in any year after calendar year 19XX, the Paragraph 9 Vesting Factor shall be as follows: 0.0 during the period on and after the date Employee shall become a shareholder of Employer (the "Commencement Date") and before the date one (1) year after the Commencement Date; 0.33 during the period on and after the date one (1) year after the Commencement Date and before the date two (2) years after the Commencement Date; 0.66 during the period on and after the date two (2) years after the Commencement Date and before the date three (3) years after the Commencement Date; and 1.00 at all times thereafter.

**10. Dissolution After Termination.** In the event Employer makes an election to wind up and dissolve within sixty (60) days after the termination of Employee's employment, the provisions of Paragraphs 8 and 9 shall not apply, and in lieu thereof, Employee shall receive as termination pay the amount Employee would have received as a shareholder of Employer from any proceeds on dissolution were Employee a shareholder at the time of such dissolution less the amount, if any, received by Employee from the sale of Employee's shares of Employer pursuant to a Buy-Sell Agreement relating thereto to which Employee is a party. Such payments to Employee shall be made at the same time as payments are made to Shareholders of Employer.

**11. Health and Disability Insurance.** Employer shall provide Employee with, and shall pay all premiums on, standard group medical policies of insurance selected at the sole and absolute discretion of Employer; and, at Employer's sole discretion, Employer may provide group life insurance with benefits payable to Employee or Employee's designated beneficiary. Such policy or policies shall provide benefits in the event of Employee's death or illness and in accordance with the terms of said policy or policies. Employer, on behalf of Employee, shall pay a portion of the annual premium for a group disability policy or policies of insurance which shall be maintained by Employer, and Employee shall reimburse Employer for such payment. That portion of such group disability insurance annual premium to be so paid and reimbursed (the "Employee's Disability Insurance Premium Share") shall be proportional to the disability benefits available to Employee under such group policy. Such disability policy or policies shall be selected at the sole and absolute discretion of Employer with benefits payable to Employee in the event of Employee's disability in accordance with the terms of said policy or policies. Employee hereby authorizes Employer to withhold from payments otherwise due to Employee hereunder the amount of the Employee's Disability Insurance Premium Share and to apply such amount so withheld to Employee's obligation to reimburse Employer for payment of such amount on behalf of Employee.

**12. Records.** Employee agrees that on termination of Employee's employment for any reason, Employee shall not be entitled to remove or retain Employer's records or files related to any client unless the client shall specifically request that such client's records and/or files be transmitted to Employee, nor shall Employee be entitled to remove or retain any other files, figures, letters, records, papers, drawings, agreements, client lists, or copies thereof, or other confidential information of any type or description, without Employer's prior written consent.

*FOR DISCUSSION PURPOSES ONLY*

**13. Expenses.**

*A.* Employer shall provide appropriate facilities and equipment to enable Employee to perform Employee's duties hereunder and shall pay all reasonable expenses for supplies, professional license fees, and dues. Employer shall purchase appropriate comprehensive public liability, property damage, and malpractice insurance naming both Employer and Employee as insureds, covering Employer's premises and Employer's business.

*B.* Additionally, Employee shall be entitled to reimbursement from Employer for educational expenses approved by Employer incurred to maintain or improve Employee's professional skills, and for Employee's actual expenses for travel, room, and meals for attending conferences and annual meetings of professional associations when approved by Employer.

*C.* Employee shall, as a practicing CPA, incur and personally pay certain expenses other than those specified above for which Employer shall be under no obligation to reimburse or otherwise compensate Employee. These include but are not limited to professional expenses, home telephone bills, club dues, and membership expenses in civic groups and social organizations. In addition, as a condition of Employee's employment, Employee shall furnish and maintain an automobile for use in Employer's business. Nothing in this Paragraph shall prevent Employer from assuming to pay or reimbursing Employee for any expenses in any of the categories enumerated above.

**14. Life Insurance.** In addition to any insurance maintained by Employer for Employee's benefit, Employer shall have the right to obtain and maintain life insurance or other insurance with respect to Employee, at Employer's sole cost and expense and for Employer's sole benefit, and Employee shall not have any rights in or to such insurance or the proceeds thereof. Employee agrees to cooperate with Employer in obtaining such insurance and shall timely submit to the usual medical and other examinations required in connection therewith.

**15. Arbitration.** Employer and Employee agree that any unresolved dispute that may arise under the provisions of this Agreement shall be submitted to arbitration in accordance with the provisions of Paragraph 20 of a Buy-Sell Agreement between Employer and its shareholders of even date.

*FOR DISCUSSION PURPOSES ONLY*

**16. No Acts Contrary to Law.** Nothing contained in this Agreement shall be construed to require the commission of any act contrary to law, and whenever there is any conflict between any provision of this Agreement and any statute, law, ordinance, or regulation contrary to which the parties have no legal right to contract, then the latter shall prevail; but in such event, the provisions of this Agreement so affected shall be curtailed and limited only to the extent necessary to bring it within the legal require-ments. Each and all of the several rights and remedies provided for in this Agreement shall be construed as being cumulative, and no one of them shall be deemed to be exclusive of the others or of any right or remedy allowed by law. No waiver by Employer or Employee of any failure by Employee or Employer, respectively, to keep or perform any covenant or condition of this Agreement shall be deemed to be a waiver of any preced-ing or succeeding breach of the same or other covenant or condition.

**17. Notice.** All notices and demands of every kind shall be personally delivered or sent by first class mail to the parties at such addresses as either party may designate in writing. Any such notice or demand shall be effective immediately upon personal service or three (3) days after deposit in the United States mail, as the case may be.

**18. Attorneys' Fees.** In the event that any party institutes suit against any others to enforce any of the terms of this Agreement, the prevailing party in any such action shall, in addition to all other damages, be entitled to recover attorneys' fees.

**19. Covenants and Conditions.** Should any covenant, condition, or other provision of this Agreement be held by a court of competent jurisdic-tion to be invalid, illegal, or unenforceable by reason of any rule of law or public policy, all other covenants, conditions, and provisions of this Agree-ment shall, nevertheless, remain in full force and effect. No covenant or provision hereof shall be deemed dependent upon any other covenant or provision unless so expressed herein.

**20. Miscellaneous.**

A. This Agreement shall be deemed entered into in the State of _____ and shall be governed and construed in accordance with the internal laws of the State of _____ applicable to contracts made and to be performed in _____ . A waiver of any term or condition of this Agreement shall not be construed as a general waiver by Employer, and Employer shall be free to reinstate any such term or condition with or without notice to the Employee.

B. It is hereby agreed that Employee's and Employer's rights and obligations under this Agreement are personal and not assignable. This Agreement contains the entire agreement and understanding between the parties to it with respect to the matters covered hereby, supersedes all prior agreements, negotiations and discussions, and shall be binding on and inure to the benefit of the heirs, personal representatives, successors, and assigns of the parties, subject, however, to the restrictions on assignment contained herein.

C. Except as expressly provided in this Agreement, on termination Employee shall be entitled to receive only the compensation accrued but unpaid as of the termination date, plus such Employee's termination pay as provided in Paragraph 8 or 9, but shall not be entitled to any additional compensation.

D. This Agreement may not be altered, modified, amended, changed, rescinded, or discharged in whole or in part except by a writing executed by the parties hereto.

E. The paragraph headings used in this Agreement are for reference and convenience only and shall not in any way limit or amplify the terms and provisions hereof or enter into the interpretation of this Agreement.

F. Employee and Employer represent and warrant that they are free to enter into this Employment Agreement and that they have not made and shall not hereafter make any agreement or commitment in conflict with the conditions hereof or which could or might interfere with the rendition of their services and duties hereunder. Employee agrees to indemnify Employer, and Employer agrees to indemnify each Employee, and they each agree to hold each other harmless from and against any loss, liability, judgment, cost, or expense of any kind and character suffered or incurred by the respective parties by reason of any breach of any of the foregoing warranties by Employee or Employer.

G. Employer agrees to include Employee as a participant in any Qualified Employee Benefit Plan established by the Employer.

*FOR DISCUSSION PURPOSES ONLY*

IN WITNESS WHEREOF, Employer has caused this Agreement to be executed by its duly authorized officer and each Employee has executed this Agreement effective _____, 19XX.

A Professional Corporation
"Employer"

By: _____
    Vice President


_____
"Employee"

*The illustrative material below has been included for informational purposes only. Practitioners who feel that any of this material would be useful in their own agreements are advised to consult legal counsel for specific advice on the appropriateness and effect of such use.*

# Buy-Sell Agreement

THIS AGREEMENT is made as of _____, 19XX, by and between _____ and all other persons who may hereafter execute this Agreement as a shareholder (which such persons are hereinafter referred to individually as a "Shareholder" and collectively as the "Shareholders") and _____, a Professional Corporation duly organized under the laws of the State of _____ (hereinafter referred to as the "Company").

RECITALS

A. The Shareholders are the sole Shareholders of the Company, owning all of the issued and outstanding shares of the capital stock of the Company (the "Company Stock"); and

B. The parties to this Agreement deem it to be in their best interest, for their mutual protection and the more harmonious and successful management of the Company, to provide for the purchase and sale of the shares of stock, both during the life of each Shareholder and upon a Shareholder's death; and

C. The Shareholders are required to provide for the repurchase of shares of stock of the Company under the rules promulgated pursuant to _____ Corporations Code Section _____;

NOW, THEREFORE, in consideration of the premises and the benefits to be derived from the mutual observance of the covenants contained herein, the parties do hereby bind themselves, their respective heirs, executors, administrators, and assigns and agree as follows:

**1. Restrictions on Transfer of Shares.** No Shareholder may sell, transfer, assign, hypothecate, pledge, mortgage, give, or otherwise dispose of or in any way alienate or encumber any shares of the Company or any rights or interest therein, except as set forth herein.

*FOR DISCUSSION PURPOSES ONLY*

**2. Option to Purchase Stock.** If any Shareholder desires to sell, assign, hypothecate, pledge, mortgage, or otherwise alienate or encumber any Company Stock, all Company Stock owned by said Shareholder must first be offered to the Company, and the Company shall have the option hereinafter set forth:

A. Unless waived by the Company and all Shareholders, there can be no valid sale, assignment, hypothecation, pledge, mortgage, or other alienation or encumbrance of less than all a Shareholder's Company Stock; and unless so waived, transfers of less than all of a Shareholder's interest in such Shareholder's Company Stock are strictly prohibited.

B. If a Shareholder desires to transfer all of such Shareholder's shares of Company Stock, such Shareholder (the "Offering Shareholder") shall deliver a notice in writing, by mail, to the Secretary of the Company and to the other Shareholders of such Offering Shareholder's shares. Promptly upon receipt of such notice, the Secretary shall give notice of the Offering Shareholder's intention to the Directors of the Company. Within ten (10) days after said notice has been received by said Secretary, a special meeting of the Board of Directors of the Company shall be duly called, noticed, and held for the purpose of considering the proposed transfer. For twenty (20) days following receipt of such notice by the Secretary, the Company shall have the option to purchase all of the Offering Shareholder's shares of Company Class A and Class B Stock at the price per share set forth in Paragraph 4 hereof, payable in full ninety (90) days after the date such option is exercised.

C. The option set forth in Subparagraph B shall be exercised by written notice to the Offering Shareholder. The stock certificate representing the offered shares shall be delivered to the Company at the time of closing, duly endorsed for transfer.

D. In the event the Company does not exercise the option set forth in Subparagraph B hereof so that all of the stock of the Offering Shareholder is purchased, the Company forthwith shall be dissolved and liquidated.

**3. Termination of Employment.**

A. In the event of the termination of any Shareholder's employment with the Company for any reason other than death, such event shall constitute an offer to sell all of the Class A and Class B Stock of such Shareholder at the price per share set forth in Paragraph 4 hereof and upon all the terms and conditions contained in Paragraph 2. Upon the effective date of termination of employment, the Secretary or any other officer of the Company shall call a meeting of the Board of Directors as provided in Paragraph 2 of this Agreement. Notwithstanding anything herein contained to the contrary, any such sale shall close not later than ninety (90) days after the selling Shareholder ceases to be a licensed person or becomes a disqualified person.

B. Upon the death of any Shareholder, the estate of such Shareholder shall sell and the Company shall purchase all of the shares of Class A and Class B Stock then owned by such Shareholder at the price provided in Paragraph 4.

C. If the Company fails to purchase said shares of stock as required by Paragraph 3A or 3B above, the Company shall be dissolved and liquidated forthwith. The stock certificate or certificates representing such shares shall be delivered to the Company at the time of closing, duly endorsed for transfer, and accompanied by an order of the Court having jurisdiction over the estate of the deceased Shareholder authorizing said sale. The sale shall be closed as soon as possible after the purchase price has been determined, but not later than ninety (90) days after the death of the Shareholder. The Company shall pay the purchase price in full on the closing date.

### 4. Purchase Price.

A. The purchase price per share of any shares of Class A Stock purchased and sold pursuant to this Agreement shall be one dollar ($1.00) per share. The purchase price per share of any shares of Class B Stock purchased and sold pursuant to the provisions of this Agreement shall be the "adjusted cash basis book value" of the Company divided by the total number of shares of Class B Stock (including those to be purchased outstanding prior to such purchase). The purchase price shall be determined in accordance with generally accepted accounting practices, subject to the provisions of this Paragraph; and such determination shall be conclusive and binding upon the parties. The purchase price shall be computed as of the last day of the calendar month immediately preceding the month in which occurs the event giving rise to the option or obligation to purchase, except that in the event of purchase due to the termination of any Shareholder's employment as a result of such Shareholder's permanent disability (as that term is defined in the Employment Agreement), the purchase price shall be determined as of the last day of the calendar month immediately preceding the commencement of such Shareholder's disability.

*B.* As used herein, "adjusted cash basis book value" refers to book value as determined using the cash receipts and disbursements method of accounting, adjusted to include as liabilities the following: (1) all accrued operating expenses of _____ , (2) sums owing to former employees under this Buy-Sell Agreement constituting the purchase price of stock of _____ , and (3) accrued contributions to the Company's Pension and Profit-Sharing Plan (if any) relating to persons other than Shareholder, but excluding any value for the life insurance policies carried by the Company pursuant to Paragraph 9 of this Agreement, fees receivable, and goodwill.

*C.* As used herein, "Employment Agreement" shall mean the agreement between each Shareholder and the Company entitled "Employment Agreement" of even date herewith.

*D.* Notwithstanding anything contained herein to the contrary, no income attributable to services rendered by the Company after any time any Shareholder becomes a disqualified person as defined in _____ Corporation Code Section _____ shall be considered in determining the value of such Shareholder's stock.

**5. Termination of Voting Rights.**   No Shareholder or any personal representative of any Shareholder shall have any voting or other rights from or after the date of such Shareholder's death, disqualification, or termination of employment with the Company.

**6. Notices.**   All notices and demands of every kind shall be personally delivered or sent by first class mail to the parties at the addresses appearing at the end of this Agreement or at such other addresses as either party may designate in writing, delivered or mailed in accordance with the terms hereof. Any such notice or demand shall be effective immediately upon personal service or three (3) days after deposit in the United States Mail, as the case may be.

**7. Enforcement of Contract.**   Shares of Company Stock cannot be readily purchased or sold in the open market, and for that reason, among others, the parties shall be irreparably damaged in the event this Agreement is not specifically enforced. If any dispute arises concerning the sale or disposition of any stock, an injunction may be issued restraining any such sale or disposition pending the determination of such controversy. In the event of any controversy, such rights or obligations shall be enforceable in a Court by a decree of specific performance. Such remedy shall, however, be cumulative and not exclusive and shall be in addition to any other remedy which the parties may have. In the event any party hereto institutes legal action or cross-action for breach or enforcement of the terms hereof, the prevailing party shall recover reasonable attorneys' fees as fixed by the Court, together with Court costs.

**8. Intent of Parties.** It is the intention of the parties to this Agreement that this Agreement shall comply with the requirements of the provisions of the _____ Business and Professions Code and the _____ Corporation Code regulating professional corporations, and the rules of the State Board of Public Accountancy. Any provision in this Agreement inconsistent with such laws, rules, or regulations shall be invalid.

**9. Life Insurance.** The Company may, at its option, carry life insurance policies on the life of any Shareholder to provide the Company with sufficient funds to enable it to purchase such Shareholder's stock pursuant to the provisions of Paragraph 3 hereof. The Company shall own all such policies and each Shareholder waives any rights such Shareholder may have under such policies. With respect to the purchase by the Company of insurance policies acquired pursuant to this Paragraph, each Shareholder specifically agrees to cooperate fully with the Company and the insurer in obtaining and maintaining such insurance on such Shareholder's life and shall timely submit to any requested medical or other examinations in connection therewith. The Company shall pay all premiums on any such insurance policies. If any Shareholder sells such Shareholder's shares in the Company during such Shareholder's life, or if this Agreement is terminated for any reason set forth in Paragraph 11 of this Agreement, the selling Shareholder (in the event of a sale during a Shareholder's life) and each Shareholder (in the event of termination of this Agreement pursuant to Paragraph 11) shall have the right to purchase any such policy or policies upon such Shareholder's life owned by the Company. The purchase price for the policy or policies shall be the interpolated terminal reserve value of such policy or policies as of the date of sale, less any existing indebtedness against such policy or policies, plus that portion of the premium or premiums on such policy or policies paid prior to the date of sale which covers the period beyond the date of sale. If such policy is term life insurance, said policy shall be transferred to the insured upon adjustment between the parties of premium paid beyond the date of sale. Such right of purchase must be exercised by the insured within ninety (90) days after sale of such Shareholder's shares or the termination of this Agreement. If not so exercised, such right shall terminate. Upon the exercise of such right, the Shareholder shall deliver the purchase price of the policy or policies on such Shareholder's life to the Company, and the Company shall simultaneously execute and deliver to such Shareholder all the documents which are required to transfer ownership of the policy or policies. If such right of purchase is not exercised within the time prescribed by this Paragraph, the Company may make whatever disposition of the policy or policies the Company shall deem proper.

**10. Endorsement.** Each stock certificate presently owned by each Shareholder and all stock certificates acquired by each Shareholder during the term of this Agreement shall bear the following endorsement:

> This certificate may be sold or transferred only upon compliance with the terms and conditions of the Buy-Sell Agreement dated _____, 19XX, among _____, a Professional Corporation (the "Company") and the shareholders of the Company, a copy of which is on file with the Secretary of the Company.

**11. Termination.** This Agreement shall terminate upon the occurrence of any of the following events:

*A.* Bankruptcy, receivership, or dissolution of the Company

*B.* The purchase of the Company's stock so that there remains but one shareholder

*C.* The written agreement of the holders of seventy-five percent (75%) of the outstanding Class B shares of the Company

**12. New Shareholders.** In the event any person desires to acquire stock in the Company, the Company shall require such person, as a condition of such person's acquisition of stock in the Company, to execute this Agreement. In the event any such person does not promptly execute this Agreement, the Company shall not issue any Company stock to such person.

**13. Entire Agreement.**  This Agreement constitutes the entire agreement of the parties hereto with respect to the matters set forth herein and supersedes all prior agreements, negotiations, concurrent representations, or promises of any party hereto or any of their respective agents or representatives. This Agreement may not be altered, modified, amended, changed, rescinded, or discharged, in whole or in part, except by a writing executed by all the parties hereto.

**14. Covenants and Conditions.**  Should any covenant or other provision of this Agreement be held by a court of competent jurisdiction to be invalid, illegal, or unenforceable by reason of a rule of law or public policy, all other conditions and provisions of this Agreement shall nevertheless remain in full force and effect. No covenant or provision hereof shall be deemed dependent upon any other covenant or provision unless so expressly stated herein.

**15. [State] Law to Govern.**  This Agreement shall be deemed entered into in [State], shall be governed and construed in accordance with the internal laws of [State] applicable to contracts made and/or to be performed in [State].

**16. Attorneys' Fees.**  In the event any party hereto institutes a suit or an arbitration or proceeding against any others to enforce any of the terms of this Agreement, the prevailing party in any such action shall, in addition to all other damages, be entitled to recover such party's attorneys' fees.

**17. Paragraph Headings.**  The paragraph headings in this Agreement are for reference and convenience only and shall not in any way limit or amplify the terms and provisions hereof or affect the interpretation of this Agreement.

**18. Miscellaneous.**  This Agreement shall inure to the benefit of and be binding upon the heirs and personal representatives of each Shareholder and the successors and assigns of the Company, subject to the restrictions upon assignment set forth herein. Time is agreed to be of the essence.

**19. Arbitration.**  It is the intent of the parties that any and all disputes hereunder shall be subject to arbitration as provided in Section _____ of the _____ Code of Civil Procedure. Notwithstanding any provisions of the aforesaid rules or statutes to the contrary, the refusal or failure of any party to appear or participate in any hearing or other portions of any

*FOR DISCUSSION PURPOSES ONLY*

arbitration proceeding pursuant to this Section shall not prohibit such arbitration hearing from proceeding, and the arbitrator is empowered to make a decision and/or render an award ex parte which shall be binding on each party as fully as though such party had participated fully in each hearing or proceeding. The prevailing party in any arbitration proceeding or legal proceeding to enforce arbitration shall be entitled to recover in addition to all of the damages the prevailing party's reasonable attorneys' fees.

IN WITNESS WHEREOF, the parties have caused this Agreement to be executed as of the date first written above.

_____
Shareholder

A Professional Corporation
(the "Company")

By_____
    President

SPOUSE'S CONSENT

I acknowledge that I have read the foregoing Buy-Sell Agreement (the "Agreement") and know its contents. I am aware that under the Agreement my spouse agrees to sell all of my spouse's interest in the Company, including my community interest therein, upon my spouse's death, total disability, voluntary withdrawal or involuntary withdrawal. I further understand that by the terms of the Agreement, my spouse agrees to limitations upon my spouse's right to sell my spouse's interest in the Company voluntarily during my spouse's life. I hereby consent to such sale and such limitations, approve the provisions of said Agreement, and agree that I shall not bequeath said interest in the Company or any portion thereof or any interest therein by my Will, if I predecease my spouse. I direct that the residuary clause in my Will shall not be deemed to apply to my community interest in the Company.

_____
Spouse's Signature

          Dated:_____, 19XX

*FOR DISCUSSION PURPOSES ONLY*

# Services and Publications of the Management of an Accounting Practice Committee

**National Practice Management Conferences,** targeted toward managing partners of local firms, offer a practical approach to practice management. Geared to mid-size and larger local firms, but open to all. Two each year: summer and fall. (212) 575–3814

**National Small Firm Conferences,** designed for sole practitioners and firms with two to four partners, provide practical guidance on how to operate a successful, small firm. As with all MAP conferences, exchange of information on management problems and solutions with other practitioners is emphasized. Two conferences annually: summer and fall.
(212) 575–3814

**National Marketing Conferences** are for firms of all sizes but are designed primarily for partners responsible for marketing and Marketing Directors. The conferences cover techniques for successful practice development. One annually in June. (212) 575–3814

*MAP Handbook,* a comprehensive 1,000 page, three-volume, looseleaf reference service on practice management, is updated annually. It includes more than 200 forms, sample letters, checklists, worksheets, all easy to reproduce or adapt for your practice needs. It provides detailed financial data and policy information for various-sized firms that enable you to evaluate your performance with comparable-sized firms. Topics covered include developing an accounting practice, administration, personnel, partnerships, and management data.

For Information (212) 575–3826
To Order 1–800–323–8724

*MAP Selected Readings,* a companion book to the *MAP Handbook,* is a reader's digest of over 500 pages of articles on successful practice management, specially compiled from leading professional journals. The articles contain numerous profit-making ideas for your practice. A new *Selected Readings* edition is published annually.

For information (212) 575–3826
To order 1–800–323–8724

115

**MAPWORKS—DOCUMAP** contains documents from the **MAP Handbook** dealing with organization, client engagements, and personnel on diskette. Available in three formats: APG2–No. 016911, ASCII–No. 090080, and WordPerfect 4.2–No. 090081.

|  |  |
|---|---|
| U.S. | 1–800–334–6961 |
| New York State | 1–800–248–0445 |
| Outside U.S. | (212) 575–7017 |

**On Your Own! How to Start Your Own CPA Firm** provides nuts-and-bolts advice on how to start a CPA firm. It contains a wealth of hands-on information on operating profitably that would be useful to both new and existing firms as well as prospective firm owners.

|  |  |
|---|---|
| U.S. | 1–800–334–6961 |
| New York State | 1–800–248–0445 |
| Outside U.S. | (212) 575–7017 |

Other MAP Committee publications will be published in the future, including an upcoming guide on practice continuation agreements, a must for sole practitioners and other small firms. Watch AICPA ''Update'' for announcements of publication dates.

The **MAP Inquiry Service** responds to member inquiries concerning firm management and administration. Need more help? The MAP staff can put you in touch with experienced CPAs or consultants who can assist you with your special problems.      (212) 575–3814

The **MAP Roundtable Discussion Manual** contains guidelines for organizing a MAP roundtable discussion group. Such a group helps firms find practical solutions to common issues or problems through regular meetings and information exchange. The guidelines include sample correspondence, forms to administer a roundtable, and twenty suggested discussion outlines on topical management issues.      (212) 575–3814

# About the Author

Mark F. Murray is an honors graduate of Merrimack College and Suffolk University Law School in Boston, where he concentrated in accounting and corporate law. Prior to joining the staff of the AICPA Industry and Practice Management Division, Mr. Murray practiced law and managed the accountant's professional liability program for a prominent insurance company. Mr. Murray is an editor and contributing author of the AICPA *Management of an Accounting Practice Handbook*.

# Index